YALE HISTORICAL PUBLICATIONS

WALLACE NOTESTEIN ESSAYS, 4

DAVID HORNE, EDITOR

PUBLISHED UNDER THE DIRECTION
OF THE DEPARTMENT OF HISTORY

NEW HAVEN AND LONDON, YALE UNIVERSITY PRESS, 1964

Gaddis Smith

BRITAIN'S

CLANDESTINE

SUBMARINES

1914-1915

Preface

I came upon the trail of Britain's clandestine submarines while gathering material for a larger study (soon to be completed) on the relations of the United States, Great Britain, and Canada in the era of the First World War. At first the submarines seemed worth no more than a footnote, but soon an extraordinary volume of information about them began to accumulate as the unexpected by-product of other inquiries. It became obvious that what had appeared as an uncomplicated episode was actually the center of a web of events which illustrated many of the general historical conditions with which I was concerned. The book that has resulted is presented both for its own sake and as a contribution to what John Bartlet Brebner called in his pioneering study the *North Atlantic Triangle: The Interplay of Canada, the United States, and Great Britain* (New Haven, 1945).

This book could not have been written without the help of many individuals and institutions. Samuel Flagg Bemis, mentor and colleague, attracted me to the study of diplomatic history and inspired my interest in the North Atlantic Triangle. Many scholars at Yale and elsewhere made valuable suggestions in conversation or correspondence. I would like to give special thanks to John M. Blum, Eugene Forsey, Arthur S. Link, Arthur J. Marder, Ernest R. May, C. P. Stacey, Richard H. Ullman, and Robin W. Winks. Research was a pleasant adventure because of the unfailing helpfulness and good spirits of the staff members of the Yale and Duke University Libraries, the Library of Congress Division of Manuscripts, the National Archives, the Public Archives of Canada, and the Bodleian Library, Oxford University. I am indebted to R. W. Mason, librarian of the Foreign Office, for permission to consult the Grey and Spring-Rice papers for years prior to 1915. James M. Packham of Canadian Vickers, Ltd., was a gracious and informative host during my visit to the Company's plant in Montreal, as was J. D. Scott, historian of Vickers, Ltd., during my visit to Vickers House, London. I wish to thank E. T. Moffett of the Bethlehem Steel Company for permission to see and use copies of the all-important contracts pertaining to the submarines, and the General Dynamics Corporation for permission to reproduce photographs and to consult their Archives at the Submarine Library in Groton, Connecticut, where Mrs. Theda Bassett, librarian, was most helpful. I am grateful also to the Billings Fund and the Concilium on International Studies at Yale for the grants which made possible my research in England and Scotland. For special permission to consult the Asquith Papers and the Lord Fisher Papers I am indebted to Mark Bonham Carter and the Duke of Hamilton respectively. Finally, I thank David Horne, editor of Yale Historical Publications, who showed me how imperfect a supposedly "final" draft can be. Without his labors these pages would never have come into print.

G. S.

New Haven, Connecticut
May 1964

Contents

Illustrations

Britain's Clandestine Submarines, 1914-1915

1 The Setting

The First World War on the seas belonged to the U-boat, but the submarines of this book did not appreciably alter the course of combat by their operations. They were British submarines and their significance lies not in what they did but in the manner of their creation in Britain, America, and Canada at a critical time for all three countries. This clandestine affair reveals much concerning the history of American neutrality, Canadian national aspirations, and British efforts to cope with the problems posed by the war.

The opening years of the twentieth century were outwardly a genial time in the political relations of the three English-speaking countries bordering the shores of the North Atlantic. Great Britain and the United States had buried old animosities and formed an unwritten entente.[1] The United States and Canada had successfully liquidated a cluster of perennial differences involving fish, seals, boundaries, and waterways.[2] Canada, confidently sensing her young and prosperous nationhood, appeared to be joining Great Britain and the other Dominions in the creation of a vigorous new imperial relationship

1. Charles S. Campbell, Jr., has written one of the better accounts of the formation of *Anglo-American Understanding, 1898–1903* (Baltimore, 1957).
2. Descriptions of these issues and their resolution can be found in Hugh Ll. Keenleyside and Gerald S. Brown, *Canada and the United States* (rev. ed. New York, 1952).

based on the principle of cooperation and partnership, not subordination.

As public-spirited men in 1914 prepared to celebrate the hundreth anniversary of Anglo-American peace, it seemed that the United States, Canada, and Great Britain were linked in an indissoluble and mutually beneficial triangle stronger than any formal alliance because it was based on common language, culture, and values. Outward serenity, however, was belied by inward turmoil. During the final years of peace before the Great War, political life in Canada and Britain was tense and excited. Men mingled optimism with apprehension, argued with a vehemence approaching ferocity, and everywhere saw large portents in small events. Unconsciously they were undergoing an emotional preparation for war.

Throughout the British Empire men's fears and hopes were dominated by the possibility of an Anglo-German naval war and by the naval arms race, which was considered a prelude to conflict.[3] In 1911 Germany challenged France's right to hegemony in Morocco, and the British government responded with a self-righteous truculence that startled the world and precipitated a diplomatic crisis which changed the atmosphere of British foreign policy. Before 1911 an Anglo-German war had been a theoretical possibility, a plaything of the military writers and more jingoistic politicians. After 1911 such a war became a real and terrible threat. This attitude was not washed away by the months of relatively placid Anglo-German diplomacy from 1912 into the summer of 1914. The overwrought mood of 1911 became a condition. The impact on relations between mother country and the Dominions was profound. Canadians were especially disturbed.

The belief in a grave external threat to the British Empire

3. E. L. Woodward's *Great Britain and the German Navy* (London, 1935) is still useful. It was written too early to make use of unpublished archives and private papers, as has been done so brilliantly by Arthur J. Marder, *From the Dreadnought to Scapa Flow*, Vol. 1, *The Road to War, 1904–1914* (London, 1961). The Anglo-German naval armaments race is today in need of reappraisal.

raised the question of Canada's future. For decades Canadian political life had been predicated on absolute security. As long as the British Navy remained superior to any challenge, the United States was the only country capable of injuring Canada, and in the twentieth century every responsible leader considered war with the United States unthinkable. After providing for a small militia to ensure domestic tranquillity, the Canadian government could concentrate all thought and treasure on building the economy. Fear of Germany caused these assumptions to crumble. Few Canadians believed that Germany could attack the Dominion directly, for there was general unvoiced recognition that the United States in the last resort would undoubtedly protect Canada from invasion (although it was both fashionable and patriotic to proclaim in public that Canada sought no shelter under the Monroe Doctrine). But if the heart of the Empire was threatened, did not Canada have a moral duty to assist? Furthermore, if the British Navy lost control of the seas, how could the trade of the Empire, in which Canada had a direct interest, be preserved?

Both major Canadian political parties agreed that the Dominion did indeed have a duty to aid the beleaguered mother country, but they did not agree on how the duty should be fulfilled. Most Liberals argued that Canada should have a navy built in Canada, manned by Canadians, and stationed under ordinary circumstances in Canadian waters. Many Conservatives, on the other hand, declared that a few small vessels, "tinpots," far from home waters, added nothing to Britain's strength in the emergency posed by Germany's growing fleet of battleships. Conservatives declared that Canada's duty was to contribute cash for the construction in England of the largest and most powerful ships to be manned by the experienced officers and men of the Royal Navy and stationed wherever the Admiralty considered they would do the most good. This meant, according to the reigning doctrines of Alfred Thayer Mahan, that they should be kept in home waters: concentration in strength at the point of greatest peril. Liberals, in rebuttal, charged that the policy urged by Conservatives was demeaning, suitable perhaps for a colony but not for a proud self-governing Dominion.[4]

The question of Canadian self-government led directly to controversies over the nature of the imperial tie and relations with the United States. Some Conservatives looked sympathetically on the idea of a federal reorganization of the British Empire with common taxation, integrated armed forces, and some form of central executive and legislative body sitting in London. Only thus, they argued, could the Empire survive in an armed and hostile world. Without organic union Canada would become a dependency of the United States; total political absorption would inevitably follow. These ideas were assailed by Liberals and a few Conservatives. Sir Wilfrid Laurier, Liberal prime minister from 1896 to 1911, denied that Canada was in danger of being absorbed by the United States, belittled the severity of the German threat, and resisted every suggestion that even winked in the direction of imperial centralization.

In 1911 Laurier faced a crisis in which the imperial question was emotionally entangled with the future health of the Canadian economy and political relations with the United States. The specific issue was his proposed Canadian-American reciprocal trade agreement. The Conservative opposition charged that reciprocity would deprive Canada of her opportunity for industrial growth and would make her a permanently exploited producer of raw materials. The imperial tie would be forgotten; political and economic servitude to the United States would follow. The people believed enough of these dire predictions to throw out the Liberals and reciprocity.[5]

The new prime minister, Robert L. Borden (knighted in 1914), was immediately confronted with a difficult question. Was it possible to reconcile the requirements of imperial defense, which would mean a degree of subordination to Great

4. For the naval controversy in Canada see Gilbert Norman Tucker, *The Naval Service of Canada* (2 vols. Ottawa, 1952), *1*, chaps. 4–9.

5. L. Ethan Ellis, *Reciprocity, 1911* (New Haven, 1939) is adequate on the purely Canadian-American aspects of the subject, but underplays the imperial facets of the 1911 election.

Britain, with the drive for national status and industrial development, symbolized by the defeat of reciprocity? In short, were nation and empire compatible? From 1911 to 1914 Borden and many others in Canada and England sought to resolve this great uncertainty. The approach of the Great War seemed momentarily to bring relief. The editor of the *Times* in London voiced a widespread opinion when he wrote, on July 31, 1914, "the one hope I see . . . on this very black day is that it may turn us into an Empire after all."[6] Prime Minister Borden also felt a surge of imperial solidarity as he cabled to London on August 1 that "if unhappily war should ensue the Canadian people will be united in a common resolve to put forth every effort and to make every sacrifice necessary to ensure the integrity . . . of our Empire."[7] Alas, the war solved no problems. Before many weeks had gone by, Borden and the Canadian government were more harried than ever by the central issue of nation or empire. At that moment, as we shall see, they were faced with the affair of the clandestine submarines.

The American government in the years 1911 to 1914 was far less concerned with international affairs than were the countries of the British Empire. The rumbling of the Anglo-German armaments race was heard with detached alarm, but tension in Europe seemed only to demonstrate the moral superiority of the United States and the virtues of political isolation. In 1913 Woodrow Wilson entered the White House and called for a foreign policy based on moral idealism and nonentanglement. He was not tempted by the hints of his intimate adviser, Colonel Edward M. House, that the United States should intervene dramatically to avert a European and world cataclysm. Wilson believed that the duty of his country was to exert moral force by righteous example.

The outbreak of the Great War momentarily confirmed the

6. Geoffrey Robinson to Sir John Willison, Willison MSS, Public Archives of Canada, Ottawa.

7. Canada, Sessional Papers, Special Session, 1914, No. 40a, *Correspondence by Cable between the Governor-General and the Secretary of State for the Colonies, from August 1 to August 15, 1914*, 41.

apparent good sense and practicality of cool and perfect detachment. In a famous message Wilson declared that "the effect of the war upon the United States will depend upon what American citizens say and do. . . . We must be impartial in thought as well as in action, must put a curb upon our sentiments as well as upon every transaction that might be construed as a preference of one party to the struggle before another." America must be "a Nation that neither sits in judgment upon others nor is disturbed in her own counsels and which keeps herself fit and free to do what is honest and disinterested and truly serviceable for the peace of the world."[8]

Unfortunately, the war proved as inimical to perfect detachment for the United States as it did to perfect and automatic imperial unity between Canada and Britain. Even while Wilson wrote, events were proving how difficult his words were to interpret, much less to follow. What was an unneutral transaction? How could the standards of the past be applied to a war fought under technological conditions radically different from anything that had gone before? To what extent ought Americans to deny themselves economic advantages in obedience to a plea for neutral behavior that was impossible to define? Could private business interests shape the nation's behavior and ought they be allowed to do so? How far could and ought the government act when the law was silent or ambiguous? These questions provided the American setting for the episode of the clandestine submarines, as they did for other issues which, unlike the submarines, have been thoroughly and accurately ventilated by historians.[9]

Canada as a secondary participant and the United States as a neutral had to react in the autumn of 1914 to wartime situations originating elsewhere. Great Britain, as potentially the strongest member of the coalition against Germany, had to initiate action in pursuit of victory. For years before 1914 the

8. Message presented in the Senate, August 19, 1914, Woodrow Wilson, *Public Papers* (6 vols. New York, 1925-27), *3*, 157-59.
9. Nowhere in greater detail than by Arthur S. Link, *Wilson: The Struggle for Neutrality, 1914-1915* (Princeton, 1960).

British government, through the Committee of Imperial Defence, had planned for the possibility of war. Suddenly these plans had little value. On land Germany was stronger, Russia and France weaker, than anticipated. On the sea serious doubt arose as to the utility of Britain's vaunted superiority over Germany in dreadnought battleships. If naval superiority was lost, all was lost. In this moment of doubt, Admiral Lord Fisher, indefatigable advocate of the submarine as the weapon of the future, was called from retirement to take up his old post as First Sea Lord of the Admiralty. Without him the clandestine submarines would not have been born.

2 Admiral Fisher's Crusade

It is one of the ironies of naval warfare in the twentieth century that the development of the dreadnought, the all-big-gun battleship, took place simultaneously with the perfection of the submarine, the comparatively tiny and delicate instrument which, along with the airplane, made the great battleship obsolete. It is an even greater irony that the same man who, more than any other, inspired the creation of the all-big-gun battleship and inadvertently deluded the public into regarding the dreadnought as the ultimate and only standard of naval power was also among the first to foresee the revolutionary implications of the submarine. But Admiral Sir John Fisher (created Baron Fisher in 1909), having called the dreadnought into being, could not succeed in the years before the Great War in turning the attention of the public, the politicians, or his professional colleagues away from the battleship to the submarine. Nevertheless, up to and beyond the outbreak of war, Fisher never faltered in his crusade. The story of that crusade is an essential part of the background to the history of the clandestine submarines.

The submarine as a practical instrument of warfare is a weapon of the present century, and in the first decade of the century Great Britain did more than any other power to expand the submarine arm of its Navy. The introduction of the submarine to the Royal Navy was, curiously, the result of a successful chapter in Anglo-American cooperation—not at the level of governments but among private companies. The principal inventor of the modern submarine was an Irish-American named John P. Holland. The first Holland boat, *The Fenian Ram,* was built in 1875. As its name implies, it was intended (like David Bushnell's famed *Turtle* of the American Revolution) to attack the British. *The Fenian Ram* and a larger successor were, however, plagued by technical difficulties and— fortunately from the point of view of amicable Anglo-American relations—were never used in anger.[1] In the closing years of the nineteenth century Holland tried, without success, to persuade the United States Navy to purchase submarines. At this juncture a key figure appeared on the scene—Isaac L. Rice, a lawyer from Philadelphia and a successful entrepreneur in the manufacture of electric storage batteries. In 1898 Rice formed the Electric Boat Company and on February 7, 1899, purchased the Holland submarine patents. Fourteen months later, in April 1900, the United States Navy purchased its first Holland submarine from Electric Boat. Rice then extended his operation to England. Thanks to connections with the Rothschild banking house, he was able to begin negotiations with the Admiralty's blessing, reaching an important agreement with the huge British armaments and shipbuilding firm, Vickers-Maxim & Sons, Ltd. (changed in 1911 to Vickers, Ltd.). Under this agreement Vickers was granted a twenty-five-year license to manufacture submarines, with Electric Boat's Holland patents, in Great Britain. This is an example of how long before the outbreak of the Great War the industrial bonds of the North Atlantic Triangle were being tied.

Vickers' began submarine production immediately. The Admiralty proved a willing customer. By 1903 five Holland boats had been delivered, by 1905 thirteen boats in the "A" series; eleven in the "B" series followed in 1906, thirty-eight in the "C" series were delivered by 1910, followed by the larger "D" and "E" classes. On the outbreak of war in 1914 all but twelve of

1. Frank T. Cable, *The Birth and Development of the American Submarine* (New York, 1924). Cable was an active participant in many of the events he describes.

the Royal Navy's submarines had been produced by Vickers under the arrangement with Electric Boat.[2]

Meanwhile, in the United States, Electric Boat was not faring well. The American Navy, without an Admiral Fisher to goad it, had been moving less rapidly than the Royal Navy with its submarine program. According to Isaac Rice, President Theodore Roosevelt admitted privately that the Navy feared to push submarines lest Congress withhold appropriations for building battleships.[3] Similar qualms were later to plague British naval building policy. When Electric Boat grew faint from lack of orders, Vickers stepped in with cash. As early as the spring of 1902 Vickers was buying Electric Boat stock, and by the end of 1903 Vickers and Rice together held majority interest in the American company. Orders for submarines from both belligerents during the Russo-Japanese War provided only temporary resuscitation, and by 1907 Electric Boat was forced to borrow heavily from Vickers. The license holder had become master.

Electric Boat's orders from Russia and Japan were important because they were later cited as providing precedents for the submarines of 1914–15. Early in the Russo-Japanese War the Lake Torpedo Boat Company of Bridgeport, Connecticut, sold a submarine to Russia amid accusations from the American press, generally pro-Japanese in its attitude, that the sale was a violation of neutrality. Electric Boat followed by selling a single submarine, the *Fulton,* to Russia. The *Fulton* was sent under exciting circumstances. A midnight rendezvous was arranged for the submarine, a floating derrick, and a large freighter in Gardiner's Bay on Long Island Sound. The submarine was hoisted to the deck of the freighter, which then sailed for Kronstadt. Subsequently, Electric Boat sold five submarines to Japan. The five were built and then dismantled for shipment in parts. An expert from the Company accompanied the parts

2. For relations between Vickers and Electric Boat and production figures see J. D. Scott, *Vickers: A History of the Company* (London, 1963). Mr. Scott kindly allowed me to read his book in manuscript.

3. Rice to Albert Vickers, December 21, 1909, Vickers MSS, Vickers House, London.

to Japan and supervised their reassembly. At the time no one complained officially that this procedure violated American neutrality.[4]

During the years that Vickers was utilizing its rights to the Holland patents to become the foremost producer of submarines in the world and at the same time providing the financial assistance that kept the Electric Boat Company alive, Admiral Fisher was rising to the highest professional position in the British Navy. In 1902–03 he was Second Sea Lord, in 1903–04 Commander-in-Chief of the great naval establishment at Portsmouth, and in October 1904 First Sea Lord, the highest post in the Navy and one which he held until retirement in 1910 at the age of 69. Professor Marder has brilliantly and with justifiable admiration described Fisher's impact on the Navy. Under Fisher's rule the complacent, leisurely, conservative, unimaginative Navy inherited from the long dull years of the nineteenth century was ruthlessly reorganized; purged of obsolete ships, men, and methods; animated with a passion for scientific perfection; and brought to a state of instant readiness for war. Fisher's greatest achievement was, of course, the introduction of the dreadnought—the *Dreadnought* itself was commissioned in 1906—but he presided over other thoroughgoing innovations and improvements in training, gunnery, and organization. He was a disruptive force, creating great animosities as well as great loyalties; he was tactless, vengeful, prone to exaggeration, but for all his faults he got results.

While Fisher remained First Sea Lord, the submarine fleet grew with great and accelerating speed. In 1904, when the Navy possessed only the five tiny Holland boats and the first of the short-range "A" class, Fisher wrote: "I don't think it is even *faintly* realized—*the immense impending revolution which the submarines will effect as offensive weapons of war.*"[5] This was at a time when most naval thinkers held, as they continued to hold until after the outbreak of war, that the submarine was

4. Cable, *American Submarine*, pp. 216–20, 237–38, 245–47.
5. Quoted in Marder, *Road to War*, p. 332.

primarily a defensive weapon, and a not particularly reputable one at that.

After Fisher's retirement, a succession of quieter and less capable men held the post of First Sea Lord. There was a marked falling off in the momentum that up to 1910 had carried the submarine service so far. Especially after the naval scare of 1909 the public could see nothing but dreadnoughts. Even in the sanctum of the Cabinet or the Committee of Imperial Defence all discussion of comparative naval strength degenerated to an over-simplified juggling of numbers of battleships in being or projected for various years in the future. Germany, slower to embark on a submarine program than Britain, began to catch up in number of undersea vessels and to forge ahead in the all-important long-range overseas types. Fisher, in retirement, saw that the submarine was failing to win the support he deemed necessary, and at every opportunity he bombarded his naval and political friends with strident letters and memoranda. A few of the recipients became converts. Arthur Balfour, for example, agreed that the days of the dreadnought were numbered and with characteristic pessimism was even more prescient than Fisher in foreseeing the future use of the submarine. After Fisher sent a memorandum extolling the uses Great Britain might make of the submarine, Balfour replied that he was more worried by what enemy submarines might do to Britain than by what British submarines might do to the enemy. Balfour asked, "What is to prevent the Germans sealing up every port, military or commercial, round our whole coast—and this whatever our superiority in battleships and cruisers might be?"[6] Fisher was unable to answer. One of his gravest deficiencies was that he was so concerned with the offensive possibilities of submarines that he gave little thought to how to defend against them; but then neither did anyone else before 1915.

Fisher banged his publicity drum loudly but made discouragingly little progress in winning support in naval circles. Perhaps this was the penalty he had to pay for his success in winning ac-

6. Balfour to Fisher, May 6, 1913, Fisher MSS in possession of the Duke of Hamilton, Lennoxlove, Haddington, Scotland.

ceptance for the dreadnought. In the years 1910–14 the heavy-gun battleship represented orthodoxy and intellectual as well as strategic security. The dreadnought worshipers had been too well trained, and they had carried the public with them. The public loved a spectacle, and found it in the great line of battle, the parade of mighty ships smudging the sky as far as the eye could see and rattling windows all along the coast with gunnery practice. The invisible submarine could not compete with this romantic and captivating demonstration of naval power. The dreadnoughts were the Navy. What was a submarine? A tin death trap no bigger than a steamer on the upper Thames, a dirty, foul-smelling, ungentlemanly contraption which did little else than endanger the lives of its occupants. What battles had the submarine ever won? What ships had a submarine ever sent to the bottom? The submarine, in short, was an untested theory. And should it win any wide support, there was always the danger that economy-conscious politicians might successfully demand fewer dreadnoughts. This, thought the large antisubmarine faction, would be a fatal mistake.

With the weight of professional naval opinion thus luke-warm or hostile to the claims of the submarine, the attitude of the civilian head of the Admiralty, the First Lord, was of the utmost importance. The First Lord from October 1911 until May 1915 was Winston S. Churchill. Before the Agadir crisis of 1911, during which he replaced Reginald McKenna at the Admiralty, Churchill had been numbered among the "economists" in the Cabinet, that faction which questioned the high level of naval expenditures. But the Agadir crisis wrought a change in Churchill's outlook, and from the moment he became First Lord he championed the Navy's case with a fervor which even the most intemperate jingo could not criticize.

At first Churchill, in calculating comparative naval strength, was not one to challenge the orthodox dominance of the dread-nought. Before the Cabinet or when presenting the naval estimates to the House of Commons, he could and did play the old battleship numbers game with a skill that no predecessor had ever approached. But unlike some professional naval officers,

Churchill had an open mind. Significantly, he had great respect for the opinions and methods of Fisher. It is important to note that he wished to bring Fisher back as First Sea Lord, and abandoned the idea only "with a good deal of reluctance."[7] He did, however, place great value on his extensive correspondence with the retired admiral. Fisher thus may have been an influence in Churchill's growing appreciation of the submarine, although Churchill, with his devotion to the unorthodox and his fondness for scientific gimmicks, undoubtedly would have realized the value without Fisher's help.

Churchill's changing attitude can be traced year by year. In February 1912, in a memorandum circulated to the Cabinet, he showed concern for the sharp increase in submarines indirectly provided for by the new German naval law. "The numbers are not stated," he commented, "but from the fact that 121 additional executive officers are required for this service alone by 1920, we may infer that between 50 and 60 submarines are to be added."[8] Churchill was clearly showing his uneasiness over the customary habit of comparing naval strengths in terms of battleships alone. An interesting result of his alarm at the increase in German submarine strength occurred the next month, when the German ambassador in London accused the British of insincerity in withdrawing "the bargain proposed by Lord Haldane" on his mission earlier in the year. Claiming that Haldane had asked, as far as naval building was concerned, only for a retardation in the rate of construction of three battleships, the ambassador charged that the British had no reason to object to the increase in the number of German submarines. The ambassador, according to Sir Edward Grey, said it was difficult to see how this could influence the British naval budget.[9] The Germans apparently considered it unfair to depart from the

---

7. Churchill to Prime Minister Herbert Asquith, November 5, 1911, Asquith MSS, Bodleian Library, Oxford University.

8. Memorandum on the Text of the New German Navy Law, February 14, 1912, ibid.

9. Grey to Sir E. Goschen, telegram, March 6, 1912, ibid.

simplistic rule of comparing battleship strength and nothing else.

Churchill was further impressed by the potential of the submarine as a result of naval maneuvers in the summer of 1912.[10] But when Fisher, in a meeting of the Committee of Imperial Defence, claimed "absolute confidence in the power of the submarine," Churchill felt it necessary to tell the Committee that "the Board of Admiralty did not entirely accept Lord Fisher's views on submarines."[11] This was an understatement. Churchill was being pulled one way by his official advisers, another by Fisher. He had not yet committed himself wholeheartedly to either. His difficulty is illustrated, fittingly enough, by negotiations which took place with Prime Minister Borden of Canada in the summer of 1912. Borden was in the process of devising a naval policy for Canada. The dominant sentiment in his Conservative party was that Canada should make a cash contribution to Great Britain for the building of dreadnoughts. This was sound battleship orthodoxy, but Borden had promised to consult the Admiralty before announcing a policy. Thus his trip to England in 1912. At the Admiralty Borden asked for an official statement demonstrating the existence of an emergency in Britain's rivalry with Germany and explaining why Canada's help was needed in the form of cash for dreadnoughts. The new German emphasis on submarines occupied a curious position in the resulting official—and secret—statement. The Admiralty sought to build a case proving Germany's aggressive intentions, thus justifying the need for more dreadnoughts. German submarines were used to bolster the argument:

> No class of vessel yet designed belongs more naturally to the defensive than the submarine [how little the Admiralty had listened to Fisher!]; but the German development of the submarine, from all the information we can obtain,

10. Marder, *Road to War*, p. 331.
11. Minutes of the 117th Meeting of the Committee of Imperial Defence, July 4, 1912, Asquith MSS.

tends to turn even this weapon of defence into one of of-
fence by building not the small class, which would be useful for the defence of their limited coast-line, but large
submarines capable of sudden and offensive operation at a
distance from their base across the sea.[12]

To conclude from this argument that more dreadnoughts were
needed was thoroughly illogical but typical of the thought of
the Admiralty Board at that time. Whether Churchill, who
endorsed the statement without reservation, was bothered by
the lack of logic is not known. The result of the negotiations
with Borden was an agreement that the Canadian Prime Minister would ask his Parliament for cash for three dreadnoughts
to be built above and beyond those already provided for in the
Admiralty estimates. Borden subsequently argued that the British Empire faced an emergency and would be in peril without
three additional battleships.[13]

12. Memorandum on the General Naval Situation Prepared for the Information of the Right Hon. R. L. Borden, K.C., M.P., August 26, 1912,
ibid. This memorandum underwent several revisions; other copies may be
consulted in the Borden MSS, in the Public Archives of Canada, Ottawa.
The final version is printed as an appendix to Gilbert Norman Tucker's
Naval Service, 1, 394–407.
13. Even Lord Fisher, in connection with Canadian naval policy, seems
to have forgotten the submarine and to have been captivated instead by a
vision of a new type of superdreadnought. "Think," he wrote, "of H.M.S.
'Incomparable'—a 25-knot battleship that will go around the whole earth
without refueling! Imagine!!! With armament and armour *beyond dreams!*
The imagination has not yet depicted her power! 45 knots motor boats
carrying 21-inch torpedoes carried in a central tank behind 16-inch
armour. . . . I wrote last night to Winston to say I proposed in my capacity
as a private British citizen to go over . . . to get Borden to build her at
Quebec. The building yard put up by Vickers is under a guarantee to build
a Dreadnought in Canada. . . . No English Government would make this
plunge, which is why I propose going to Canada and take the Vickers
people to make their bargain for building! *Keep all sacredly private,* please,
and you had better burn this letter at once." Fisher to Lord Esher, September 4, 1912, Arthur J. Marder, ed., *Fear God and Dread Nought: The Correspondence of Admiral of the Fleet Lord Fisher of Kilverstone* (3 vols.
London, 1952–59), 2, 478.
I have not been able to discover how Churchill reacted to this burst of
imagination, but no doubt negatively, for Fisher's scheme conflicted with

By endorsing Borden's policy of contribution for three dreadnoughts, Churchill did not discuss in public the possibility that the battleship might already be obsolete, lest by so doing he embarrass Borden and even cause a political disaster for the Canadian. Nevertheless, from time to time Churchill did drop discreet hints. In March 1913 he told Parliament that "the strength of navies cannot be reckoned only in Dreadnoughts, and the day may come when it may not be reckoned in Dreadnoughts at all."[14] That summer, following the annual maneuvers, Churchill wrote to Prime Minister Herbert Asquith of growing confidence in submarines: "it was a great pity that the submarines did not actually fire, and another year we must make them do it, even if it involves some loss of torpedoes. . . . My opinion is that if the submarines had fired at these manœuvres, they would have made good their claim to an even larger toll of ships than they were credited with."[15] Churchill was referring, of course, to the use of dummy torpedoes, whose absence in the maneuvers was a measure of the handicaps under which the submarine service had to operate in their efforts for fuller recognition. The "another year" to which Churchill referred never came round. In the summer of 1914 a test mobilization of the fleet replaced the usual maneuvers, and after that came war.

Admiral Fisher's prewar crusade meanwhile was nearing a climax. In February 1914 he prepared and had printed a long secret memorandum entitled "The Oil Engine and the Submarine (A Contribution to the Consideration of future Sea

---

the agreement already reached with Borden. Fisher never made his proposed visit to Canada.

While on the subject of wild schemes, it should be recorded that one high-ranking naval officer (Admiral Sir Edmond J. W. Slade, former Director of Naval Intelligence and an otherwise intelligent man) did advise Borden that Canada should build submarines, but for use in the Great Lakes against the United States! Slade memorandum, July 1912, Borden MSS.

14. Great Britain, *House of Commons Debates,* March 26, 1913.
15. Churchill to Asquith, August 30, 1913, Asquith MSS.

Fighting)." In this paper he spelled out in italics and boldface type the essence of his thoughts. "The submarine," he wrote, "is the coming type of war vessel for sea fighting and as such should first of all be developed by that power . . . whose existence depends on the Navy." Equipped with advanced internal combustion engines, the submarine could destroy battle fleets, prevent blockade or invasion, and, used as a commerce destroyer, annihilate an enemy's commerce. Fisher ridiculed those who claimed that Germany would never use submarines to sink commerce: "there is nothing else the submarine can do except sink her captives. . . . The essence of war is violence and moderation in war is imbecility." Admitting that no defense against the submarines had yet been discovered, Fisher nevertheless was optimistic. Britain, he pointed out, was the first power to develop the submarine on a large scale. With unrelenting effort the initial lead over Germany could be maintained. Germany, he argued, with her short coastline of 114 miles would be far more vulnerable than Great Britain with her thousands of miles. He concluded with a claim based more on faith than logic and one that the coming war proved false: "the development of submarine warfare . . . cannot possibly cripple our trade to anything like the extent to which it can be made to cripple that of our enemy."[16] What Fisher ignored was that a fractional diminution in trade would be more damaging to Britain than the almost total destruction of her seaborne commerce would be to Germany.

Fisher gave wide circulation to this smoking document, and provoked considerable discussion—notably in regard to Britain's naval relations with Canada—but no concrete action. Churchill, reflecting Fisher's crusade, sought in March 1914 to free himself from the pledge to Canada that more dreadnoughts were the first requirement in meeting the "emergency" posed by Germany. He wrote to Borden of the shift in emphasis away from dreadnoughts and proposed that Admiral Sir John Jellicoe

16. All quotations are from "The Oil Engine and the Submarine," a secret print dated February, 1914, Fisher MSS.

visit Canada in order to suggest a new basis for Canadian naval cooperation.[17] (Borden, loath perhaps to abandon his own insistence on the absolute necessity of contributing cash for dreadnoughts, was slow to accept Churchill's proposal, and before Jellicoe could leave for Canada war broke out and the visit was canceled.) Also in March Churchill made a far stronger statement in the House of Commons than he had made the previous year. "The whole system of naval architecture and the methods of computing naval strength," he said in a clear warning to those who could see only battleships, "are brought under review by the ever growing power, radius, and sea-worthiness of the submarine . . ."[18]

In April the Earl of Selborne, a former First Lord of the Admiralty, urged Fisher on. "You must risk everything including all your power and influence with the present Government,"[19] and Fisher thereafter increased the tempo of his efforts. To the Controller of the Navy he wrote that the paucity of submarines was the "most serious thing at present affecting the British Empire."[20] He urged the Prime Minister to study his memorandum: *"We had more submarines 4 years ago when I left the Admiralty than we have now! . . .* and the Germans *then* nil. *Now* they have more high sea submarines than ourselves. . . . I have said all this to Winston till I am sick! (and made him sick too I fear!) Myself I should drop a Dreadnought secretly & go in for 20 submarines instead."[21] It may have been more than coincidence that this number, twenty, was precisely the number of submarines Fisher ordered from Bethlehem Steel when, after the outbreak of war, he at last had a chance to turn words into action.

In June the controversy which Fisher was doing his best to stimulate erupted in the press, when Admiral Sir Percy Scott, the genius of improved long-range naval gunnery, stated blunt-

17. Churchill to Borden, March 6, 1914, Borden MSS.
18. Great Britain, *House of Commons Debates,* March 17, 1914.
19. Selborne to Fisher, March 18, 1914, Fisher MSS.
20. Fisher to the Controller of the Navy, April 20, 1914, ibid.
21. Fisher to Asquith, May 8, 1914, Asquith MSS.

ly in a letter to the *Times:* "Now that submarines have come in, battleships are of no use either for defensive or offensive purposes, and, consequently, building any more in 1914 will be a misuse of money subscribed by the citizens for the defence of the Empire."[22] If one accepted Fisher's arguments, this conclusion, however unpalatable, had to be drawn. Admiral Scott was the first to do it in public. For a month thereafter a great newspaper storm raged over Scott's opinion. By far the majority of the correspondents ridiculed rather than supported what Scott, who was in effect a stalking horse for Fisher, had said. Significantly, in Ottawa Prime Minister Borden pondered Canada's future naval policy and took note.[23]

The Scott controversy marked the climax of Fisher's crusade for the submarine before the outbreak of war. Was it a success? The following figures give the answer: At the beginning of August 1914 Great Britain had sixteen submarines capable of overseas work (seven "D's" and nine new "E's"), with nineteen under construction; Germany had twenty-eight, with twenty-four under construction.[24]

For the sake of completeness it should be noted that two submarines, built in the United States, were added to the naval strength of the Empire simultaneously with Britain's declaration of war against Germany. The manner in which these submarines were acquired was highly irregular and at the same time is of importance as background for what occurred later. When, on the first of August, it appeared likely that the British Empire would soon go to war against Germany, Sir Richard McBride, the young and excitable premier of British Columbia became alarmed for the safety of his Province, and not without reason, for the Admiralty sent a warning on August 1 that a German cruiser was reported to be operating somewhere on the

22. *Times,* London (June 5, 1914).

23. See the clippings on the Scott controversy preserved in the Borden MSS.

24. Admiral of the Fleet Lord Jellicoe, *The Grand Fleet, 1914–16* (New York, 1919), p. 140.

West Coast.[25] The premier feared not only attack by German warships but also, conceivably, aggression from Japan.[26]

McBride moved quickly when he learned that there were two submarines available for purchase in Seattle, Washington. The boats had been built in the United States for Chile by the Electric Boat Company, but they had not been delivered or fully paid for because of a controversy over specifications. With a characteristic disregard of constitutional proprieties McBride purchased the submarines for the province of British Columbia in the hope that the money would be refunded by the Dominion government. The submarines left American waters early on August 5. The next day an American cruiser, exercising the "due diligence" required of a neutral to prevent the departure of warships to a belligerent, sought to intercept the submarines. The Navy was too late; the submarines had already arrived at Esquimalt.[27] In Ottawa Borden decided to buy the vessels, reimbursing British Columbia as McBride had anticipated. The Admiralty approved and advised that the presence of the vessels on the West Coast be as widely publicized as possible in order to deter any potential German attack.[28] The submarines, designated C–1 and C–2, were the first in the Canadian Navy. Until the last German raider was eliminated from the Pacific, they remained in British Columbia waters. Although they cannot properly be taken into account when comparing British and German strength in the vital theaters of war, the fanfare that accompanied their hasty acquisition served to alert Canada to the importance of undersea weapons. Furthermore, the question of United States neutrality, here so briefly raised, foreshadowed the prolonged discussions soon to take place.

25. Colonial Secretary to the Governor-General, telegram, August 1, 1914, Borden MSS.

26. In the middle of August, McBride warned Churchill—via Borden—that Japan would not hesitate to cooperate with Germany. See Borden to Churchill, telegram, August 13, 1914, Borden MSS.

27. Tucker, *Naval Service, 1,* 284–90.

28. Colonial Secretary to the Governor-General, telegram, August 9, 1914, Borden MSS.

At the Admiralty the war had removed all political impediments to pushing rapidly ahead with submarines; within two weeks of the beginning of hostilities Churchill had secured an authorization from the Cabinet to add twelve submarines to the year's naval programme.[29] The course of war in its opening stages served to complete the conversion of the First Lord to Fisher's point of view. In September a lone German submarine scored a staggering triumph by sinking three British cruisers—the Cressy, Hogue, and Aboukir—in a single engagement. The three cruisers were patrolling the Broad Fourteens, September 22 (in violation, it so happened, of orders issued by Churchill four days before) when the Aboukir was struck by a torpedo and quickly capsized; the Cressy, standing by in order to save survivors, was next struck and sank rapidly. The Hogue, last in line, stopped and was getting out her boats to search for survivors from her sister ships when two torpedoes struck the starboard engine room. Because compartment doors had been left open, the Hogue, too, sank immediately.[30] After this calamity all doubts were dispelled; Fisher's crusade was on the verge of fulfillment.

Fear of German invasion also made converts. Who could now say with absolute confidence that the dreadnought had not become an impotent giant? And if submarines could send the fleet to the bottom or force it to cower in harbors, what could prevent the Germans from transporting an invasion army to Britain's shores? The success of the German armies in Belgium and France sharpened the point of the question. One obvious answer was more submarines—British submarines—to attack the German fleet and troop transports. If Fisher was right, a sufficient number of submarines could make Britain immune from invasion.[31]

29. Asquith to King George V, August 17, 1914, Asquith MSS.

30. "Report of the Court of Enquiry into Loss of the three cruisers . . . Aboukir, Cressy, and Hogue on September 22, 1914," Asquith MSS.

31. On mounting fears of invasion compare the confident tone of the Committee of Imperial Defence memorandum of September 8, 1914 (before the loss of the three cruisers) with the subdued alarm evident in the memo-

Throughout October, Churchill cried for more submarines with an energy and perseverance that Fisher must have approved. For example, on October 13 Churchill asked the Secretary and the Third Sea Lord of the Admiralty:

> Please state exactly what is the total submarine programme sanctioned by the Cabinet or under construction in various yards. What measures can be adopted for increasing the number of submarines? Is it possible to let further contracts for submarines on a fifteen month basis? It is indispensable that the whole possible plant for submarine construction should be kept at the fullest possible pressure day and night.[32]

A few days later Churchill gave further evidence of his new outlook in a paper arguing against reliance by the Navy on mines. "The weak, passive, immobile defence of mines cannot for a moment be compared as a military measure with the *enterprising offensive of submarines.*"[33] By now the Cabinet was taking an active interest in the need for more submarines. Churchill, however, discovered that Vickers' near monopoly of submarine construction and general red tape was holding back his war program. Accordingly, on October 28, he issued another and stronger directive to his naval subordinates:

> Please propose without delay the largest possible programme of submarine boats to be delivered in from 12 to 24 months from the present time. You should assume for this purpose that you have control of all sources of manufacture required for submarines, that there is no objection to using Vickers' drawings. . . . You should exert every effort of ingenuity and organisation to secure the utmost

---

randum of October 15, 1914. See also the minutes of the 129th meeting of the C.I.D. (Home Defence Sub-Committee), October 7, 1914. All in Asquith MSS.

32. Winston S. Churchill, *The World Crisis* (4 vols. London, 1923–29), *1*, 496.

33. Memorandum by Churchill, October 18, 1914, Asquith MSS.

possible delivery. . . . The Cabinet must be satisfied that
the absolute maximum output is being worked to in submarines. We may be sure that Germany is doing this. [We]
must not be deterred by the kind of difficulties which ham-
per action in time of peace.[34]

At the very moment Churchill was ordering a crash program
on submarines, he was forced to find and appoint a new First
Sea Lord. The pressure of public opinion against First Sea
Lord Prince Louis of Battenberg because of his German birth
was too great to resist. Battenberg's resignation was accepted
on October 29.[35] The Prince was an able and admired naval
officer, but he lacked the ruthlessness, the contempt for the
orthodox, the capacity for instantaneous action which the situation demanded.

One man possessed these qualities in full measure: Fisher.
On October 30 Churchill turned to the old warrior and invited
him back to the Admiralty as First Sea Lord. Fisher accepted.
One of his first tasks was to "exert every effort of ingenuity and
organisation to secure the utmost possible delivery" of submarines. Fisher was at last in a position to fulfill his crusade.
For the next strand in our story we must cross the Atlantic.

34. Churchill, *World Crisis, 1,* 496.
35. Mark Kerr, *Prince Louis of Battenberg* (London, 1934), p. 247. Kerr
makes the undocumented assertion that Battenberg was one of the few
senior naval officers to have an adequate appreciation of the submarine. If
this was so, Battenberg was singularly unwilling or unsuccessful in using
his position as First Sea Lord to advance the submarine service.

3 Charles Schwab's Contract

Once Admiral Fisher, on a visit to the United States, was given a supply of adhesive labels bearing in large black letters on a crimson background the word RUSH. "You stick it on a letter or a slow fool," Fisher wrote in delight. Later he used the episode of the labels to explain why his "very best friends" were Americans.[1] The spirit of the RUSH label typifies Charles Michael Schwab, president and chairman of the board of the Bethlehem Steel Corporation.

Schwab always appeared somewhat larger than life. Belonging to the tradition of Carnegie, Rockefeller, and Ford but with a pyrotechnic quality that was peculiarly his own and that linked him as much with the twentieth-century age of publicity as with the earlier age of self-made men, he was the industrial mogul in the grand style. In many ways Schwab and Fisher were very much alike, although Schwab made fewer enemies. Both demanded to be the center of every enterprise in which they participated; both had copious memories and an infinite grasp of details as well as a penchant for grand visions; both attracted newspaper reporters like small boys to a circus, and both reveled in the role of oracle: Schwab for steel, Fisher for naval weapons. Thus it is hardly surprising that the transaction concluded between them bears the imprint of their similar personalities.

1. *The Meditations of Lord Fisher* (privately printed), Fisher MSS, Lennoxlove.

At the peak of his career Schwab wrote a little book of advice, *Succeeding with What You Have.* Its maxims seem threadbare today, when the businessman has ceased to be society's hero, but one or two are worth quoting because for Schwab they were guides for action. "If more persons would get so enthused over their day's work that some one would have to remind them to go out to lunch there would be more happiness in the world and less indigestion." Another gives Schwab's views on higher education as well as business method: "college men are likely to think their evenings are meant for music, society, the theater, rather than for study that will add to their business knowledge."[2]

Schwab, born in 1862, was a prodigy in the steel industry. Starting as a dollar-a-day engineer's helper in Andrew Carnegie's J. Edgar Thomson Works, he quickly attracted Carnegie's attention because of his energy, imagination, and extrovert personality. At the age of 25 he was superintendent of the Homestead Works; at 27 he succeeded the famous Captain William R. Jones as superintendent of the Thomson Works. At 29, having restored order after the bloody Homestead strike, he was manager of both plants; and at 35 he was earning a million dollars a year as president of the Carnegie Steel Company. In 1901 Schwab was a principal intermediary in the negotiations between Carnegie and J. P. Morgan which led to the sale of Carnegie's properties and the formation of the U. S. Steel Corporation. At 39 Schwab was United States Steel's first president, earning two million dollars a year. But in 1903 Schwab resigned, as a result of friction with Judge Elbert Gary, chairman of the board. It was not enough to be president of the world's largest corporation if he could not be in supreme command.

Schwab's goal was the creation of a giant steel company which would be in every detail a reflection of his own personality and methods. That goal was to be achieved with the formation of the Bethlehem Steel Corporation, in December 1904. The nucleus of the Corporation was the Bethlehem Steel Com-

2. *Succeeding with What You Have* (New York, 1917), pp. 10–11, 34.

pany, a concern which had its origins as an iron producer during the Civil War and which at the beginning of the twentieth century was a moderately large firm specializing in the manufacture of armor plate. In 1902 the Steel Company was absorbed, by a typical exercise in corporate legerdemain, into a large and financially unsound organization known as the United States Shipbuilding Company. The Bethlehem Steel Company was the only sound unit in an institution that consisted largely of watered stock and unfounded expectations. The United States Shipbuilding Company collapsed almost immediately into bankruptcy, whereupon, in 1904, Schwab formed the Bethlehem Steel Corporation out of the wreckage.

The heart of the Corporation was the Bethlehem Steel Company, with its plant in South Bethlehem, Pennsylvania, and large iron ore deposits in Cuba. In addition, the Corporation owned eight other concerns of assorted size and value, the most important of which was the Union Iron Works in San Francisco, a shipbuilding concern. Schwab was president, chairman of the board, and largest stockholder in the Corporation.

In the decade between the formation of the Corporation and the outbreak of the World War, Bethlehem Steel grew steadily. Although Schwab developed a profitable sideline in the manufacture of ordinary commercial steel, especially girders for buildings and bridges, he concentrated his energy on the production and sale of armaments. Traveling incessantly, he was his firm's best salesman. Wherever there was war, revolution, or martial ambition, Schwab could be found: China, Europe, the Middle East, Latin America, Washington. Before the outbreak of the Great War he had sold warships to a score of countries, including the United States, Chile, Greece, Russia, Argentina, Italy, and Turkey. The combination of Schwab's leadership, the company's long experience as an armament producer, and the rapidly accelerating rate of naval expenditure around the world led to steadily rising earnings. Profits were put into rapid plant-expansion rather than dividends. The highlights of the prewar decade were the signing of a ten-million-dollar contract with Argentina (1910), the acquisition of ore

deposits of extraordinarily high quality in Chile (1912), and the
purchase of the Fore River Shipbuilding Company in Quincy,
Massachusetts (1913). With the Fore River acquisition Bethlehem had major facilities for building warships on both oceans.[3]

The years 1913 and 1914 in general were slow for the American steel industry. Railroad construction in North America had
been virtually completed and the economy as a whole seemed
to be slipping off into a depression. Feuding between business
and the Wilson administration in Washington did not contribute to confidence in the nation's economy. Bethlehem Steel,
however, was doing far better than the industry as a whole. For
example, the earnings of United States Steel fell by nearly one
third from 1912 to 1914 (from $118 million to $82 million)
while Bethlehem's nearly doubled (from $5.1 to $9.6 million).[4]
Orders for warships account for this growth in a time of general
depression. At the Fore River yards during the summer of 1914
a dreadnought was launched for Argentina while work continued on nine submarines, two torpedo boats, a submarine
tender, two large freighters, and the American battleship
Nevada.[5] Earlier in the year an order for naval guns had been
completed for Germany. In truth, no American company was
better prepared to take immediate advantage of the fast-ap-
proaching war.

With the outbreak of war Bethlehem immediately began
production on orders from the belligerents. The first orders
came from France and were for guns and artillery shells. Soon
similar orders came from Great Britain. In October Schwab,
acting as always as Bethlehem's chief salesman, sailed for England to confer with Lord Kitchener, the Secretary of State for

3. A detailed biography of Schwab has yet to be written. The article in
The Dictionary of American Biography, Supplement II, is useful. See also
Stewart Holbrook, *The Age of the Moguls* (New York, 1953), passim; the
Annual Reports of the Bethlehem Steel Corporation; and the advertisement
for the company in *Jane's Fighting Ships, 1914* (London, 1914), p. xviii.

4. From the annual Reports of the two corporations.

5. *Wall Street Journal* (June 23, 1914). This article reported that there
were more men at work in the Fore River yards than at any time in twelve
years. Sunk at Pearl Harbor, the *Nevada* was refloated in 1942.

War. In view of Bethlehem's expectations, Schwab was deliberately misleading when, on boarding the *Olympic,* he gloomily told reporters: "Conditions in the iron and steel industry are worse than I have ever seen them."[6]

The handful of passengers who accompanied Schwab on the nearly empty White Star liner *Olympic* was nervous and fearful of German attack. But for six days the voyage was uneventful. On the morning of October 27 the *Olympic* was laboring through heavy seas off the coast of Ireland. Near by was the massive British battleship *Audacious,* whose comforting presence seemed sure protection against a possible German commerce raider. Suddenly the *Audacious* shuddered from the force of a heavy explosion. She had struck a mine. As the battleship began to settle at the bow, the *Olympic* stood by, her curious and excited passengers standing along the rail. Since it appeared that the *Audacious* would not sink immediately, the *Olympic* risked collision with another mine and took the battleship in tow. The sea was too heavy, however, and the lines parted repeatedly. As night came on, the crew of the battleship was taken off. At 9 P.M. the *Audacious* blew up and sank.

From the Admiralty's point of view the battleship's loss under the eyes of the *Olympic's* passengers and crew was almost as distressing as the loss itself. If these witnesses were allowed to go ashore and report what they had seen, the damage would be serious to the Admiralty's prestige and to British morale— coming on top of the loss of the three cruisers by submarine and the more recent disastrous defeat at Coronel off the coast of Chile. Furthermore, it was highly desirable to conceal from Germany the fact that a battleship had been sunk. Beset by these dark thoughts, Admiral Sir John Jellicoe, Commander-in-Chief of the Home Fleet, determined to keep the sinking a secret. He ordered the *Olympic* detained at Lough Swilly and the passengers held without the right of communication with the shore.

6. Ibid. (October 22, 1914).

Schwab determined that this quirk of fate would not delay him. He demanded to be let off, and made such a commotion that Jellicoe himself came on board the *Olympic*. Schwab said he had an appointment with Kitchener, an urgent matter concerning munitions. Under the circumstances Jellicoe agreed to let Schwab leave the *Olympic,* but during the interview he inquired of Bethlehem Steel's facilities for building submarines. Churchill, it will be recalled, was just then issuing his October 28 order for a submarine crash program. When Schwab replied that Bethlehem could indeed build submarines, and build them fast, Jellicoe asked Schwab to call on Lord Fisher at the Admiralty. Thus the sinking of the *Audacious* by a mine became by chance a link in the history of the submarines.[7]

Traveling under the name of Alexander McDonald, Schwab arrived in London.[8] He saw Fisher at the Admiralty on November 3, whereupon occurred the breathlessly fast interview in which the submarine transaction was conceived. Fisher opened the conversation by observing that the shortest time a submarine had ever been built for the Admiralty was fourteen months. Could Schwab make delivery in six months? Schwab answered that he could do even better than that if the price were sufficiently attractive. Since cost was scarcely to be considered, agreement was reached without haggling. Schwab contracted to build twenty submarines at approximately twice the cost of the same vessels if they were to be built on a leisurely peacetime basis. In order to speed delivery the submarines were to be virtually identical with the H class boats then being built by Bethlehem and Electric Boat for the American Navy. Thus there would be no need to draw up new plans and specifications. "We have made a wonderful coup . . . with someone abroad for very rapid delivery of submarines," Fisher wrote to Admiral

7. Jellicoe, *The Grand Fleet,* pp. 149–52. There was some criticism in the Cabinet of the Admiralty's policy of concealing the loss of the *Audacious,* but the Admiralty steadfastly maintained that the Germans never knew whether the *Audacious* was sunk or merely damaged.

8. *New York Times* (November 4, 1914). Schwab loved disguise, but the press always seemed to find him out.

Jellicoe. "I must not put more on paper, but it's a gigantic deal done in five minutes. That's what I call war!"[9]

With haste all important, the Admiralty offered Schwab the use of its code room and cable facilities. An arrangement was worked out between Schwab and the chief naval censor whereby all of Schwab's messages, both incoming and outgoing, would be handled, coded, and decoded, by the Admiralty. Under this arrangement Bethlehem Steel messages were expedited throughout the war.[10]

A more cautious man than Charles Schwab would have hesitated before committing himself to build and deliver twenty submarines in the United States for a belligerent while the United States was at peace. A less confident man would have paused in the face of what on any reasonable basis would have to be considered an insuperable obstacle: to deliver vessels of war from neutral American territory for a belligerent was unequivocally against the law. For the American government to allow such delivery would be to condone the violation of a law that had existed for over 120 years, since the days when Citizen Edmond Genêt had sought to abuse the hospitality of the United States by fitting out French privateers in American waters to prey on British shipping.

The law of the United States was not the only obstacle to the delivery of Schwab's submarines. The weight of international precedent, powerfully reinforced by the decision of the Geneva tribunal in 1872, in the matter of the *Alabama* claims, opposed the agreement. During the American Civil War, it will be recalled, the Confederacy succeeded in purchasing a ship, subsequently named the *Alabama,* in England. The *Ala-*

9. For the conversation of November 3 see Fisher's *Memories and Records* (2 vols. New York, 1920), 2, 181–82. On the H class for the American Navy see John Niven, et al., *Dynamic America: A History of the General Dynamics Corporation* (New York, 1958), p. 101. Fisher's letter to Jellicoe is printed in *Fear God and Dread Nought, 3,* 66.

10. Rear-Admiral Sir Douglas Brownrigg, *Indiscretions of a Naval Censor* (New York, 1920), pp. 227–28.

bama sailed from its English shipyard in July 1862, received armament in the Azores, and proceeded on its famed career of destruction against the merchant vessels of the North. Having protested in vain against the departure of the *Alabama* from England, the American government held the British government responsible for all damages caused by the Confederate raider. The United States contended that it was the duty of a neutral government to prevent the departure from its territory of a vessel of war purchased by a belligerent. The British government, after several years of acrimonious discussion, and irresponsible talk on both sides about a war in which Canada would be captured by the United States, at length acceded to the Americans. Under the terms of the Treaty of Washington of 1871 the United States and Great Britain agreed that a neutral government was obligated to exercise "due diligence" to prevent the fitting out and departure of vessels of war for a belligerent. It was also agreed that this obligation of "due diligence" would be a governing assumption upon which a special international tribunal to convene at Geneva would determine the validity of the American claim for damages against Great Britain caused by the *Alabama* and other raiders similarly delivered into Confederate hands from British jurisdiction. The Geneva tribunal in 1872 awarded the sum of $15,500,000 to the United States.[11]

In the case of the *Alabama* the British government voluntarily accepted the American contention and assumed a legal liability in clear-thinking anticipation of a future contingency when the positions of the two nations might be reversed. If Great Britain should find herself at war (with Russia, for example) and the United States should be neutral, it would be essential to have a precedent that would prevent Britain's enemy from building potential destroyers of British commerce in the United States.[12] At the time, no one in England conceived of a situation in which Great Britain might have need

11. Samuel Flagg Bemis, *A Diplomatic History of the United States* (4th ed. New York, 1955), pp. 412–13.
12. Ibid., p. 407.

of the neutral shipbuilding facilities of the United States. But ironically in 1914, it appeared that the British government of 1871 had helped create an impossible obstacle to the delivery of the submarines so urgently demanded by the Admiralty in the war against Germany.

Schwab was not deterred. He was confident that a way around this obstacle existed. He made his verbal commitment to Fisher without hesitation and then by cable sought confirmation from international lawyers and the Department of State for a plan to deliver the submarines in parts ready for assembly. The parts would be loaded on freighters and carried to a British port, where they would be unloaded and assembled. Thus, Schwab reasoned, Bethlehem Steel would be doing no more than selling ordinary contraband. Neither American municipal nor international law would be violated. Had not American firms employed precisely this device in supplying submarines for the belligerents during the Russo-Japanese War?

Acting on Schwab's cabled instructions, Bethlehem Steel's Washington lawyer, James H. Hayden, called at the Department of State on November 5 in order to explain the proposal and to secure the Department's sanction.[13] On that day the Secretary of State, William Jennings Bryan, was home in Lincoln, Nebraska, resting after several weeks of campaigning through the West on behalf of Democratic candidates in the Congressional elections of November 3. Bryan's absence was a stroke of that good luck which appeared to be Schwab's permanent asset, for the Secretary by temperament and preconception was not likely to react favorably to the submarine scheme. First, as a sincere if somewhat inconsistent pacifist, Bryan considered all trade in war materials distasteful. If he had had his way, all export of munitions would have been embargoed. Second, the Secretary, with his midwestern agrarian roots, was highly distrustful of Great Britain. Third, he disliked legal technicalities and never regretted his deep ignorance of international law.

13. Desk diary of Robert Lansing, November 5, 1914, Lansing MSS, Division of Manuscripts, Library of Congress, Washington, D.C.

During the first month of the war Bryan's stand on the question of loans by American bankers to belligerent governments is an excellent example of his qualities as Secretary and of his emotional, intuitive, and nonlegal mind. Although there existed no legal basis on which such loans could be prohibited, Bryan argued against them on the ground that money is the worst of all contraband because it commands all others. His legally unsound argument rested on the further incorrect assumption that the sale of contraband was a violation of neutrality. President Woodrow Wilson on that occasion accepted Bryan's reasoning and the Secretary issued the statement, which was generally considered to prohibit loans to belligerents.[14]

Lawyer Hayden could hardly have anticipated much sympathy from Bryan. What the submarine scheme needed was the considerate ear of a man who knew and respected the letter of international law, admired the British cause, and had no qualms about American exports of munitions. Such a man was the Department Counselor and Acting Secretary, Robert Lansing.

When Bryan threatened an early return to Washington, Lansing had sent a telegram urging him to stay in Lincoln: "Will be glad to have you back, but my health is excellent and Department affairs are in good shape."[15] Lansing's solicitude for the Secretary barely concealed his hope that Bryan would stay away as long as possible, for without Bryan life in the Department was happier. As the chief of the Consular Bureau noted in his diary at the time: "Dept. shows absence of feverishness and more deliberation. Probably every man enjoys his work more than when the Premier is here."[16]

---

14. *New York Times* (August 16, 1914). For a discussion of this episode see Arthur S. Link, *Wilson: The Struggle for Neutrality, 1914–1915* (Princeton, 1960), pp. 62–64. It is of interest to note that Bryan, in answer to a query from a financial journalist in Toronto, declared that the ban on loans encompassed loans to Canada. Bryan to Fred W. Field, telegram, August 17, 1914, Department of State decimal file 842.51/44, Diplomatic, Legal, and Fiscal Branch, National Archives, Washington, D.C.

15. Lansing to Bryan, telegram, November 2, 1914, Lansing MSS.

16. Diary of Wilbur J. Carr, October 29, 1914, Carr MSS, Division of Manuscripts, Library of Congress.

Lansing and Bryan were opposites in almost every way. Bryan was unkempt; Lansing was meticulously groomed. Bryan was sloppy in thought and with records; Lansing was a model of efficient, precise organization. As a professional international lawyer, Lansing believed in the utility of law. He was no visionary dreaming of a utopian world rule of law, but he did feel that it was important for nations to follow international law where it existed. For Lansing the proper rule of conduct when confronting any question of foreign policy was to begin by asking what the law said. He was aware that the law might be silent or imperfect. If the latter, it was wise to follow the law while seeking improvement through orderly legal procedure.

Lansing's legal temperament as well as his general views on the neutrality policy of the United States were favorable to the submarine proposals. The Acting Secretary, for example, was concerned, as Bryan was not, over the damage that a zealously restrictive policy in regard to loans might do to American export trade. He felt that the government had a primary duty to protect and stimulate that trade in every legal way. To this end Lansing had already secured a modification of the Bryan-Wilson ban on loans. In October, while Bryan was in the West, some New York bankers had asked whether the administration would oppose short-term commercial credits, in contrast to long-term loans, extended to the Allies. Lansing endorsed the bankers' argument and wrote President Wilson that a refusal to allow credits would force foreign purchases to take their business elsewhere. "If we allow this to happen," said Lansing, "we will have neglected our foreign trade at the time of our greatest need and greatest opportunity."[17] Wilson accepted Lansing's plea, and no obstacle was placed in the way of short-term credit.

Lansing's attitude was also revealed by his relationship to the Joint State-Navy Neutrality Board, which he had created to

17. Samuel McRoberts to Lansing, October 23, 1914, and memorandum enclosed in Lansing to Wilson, October 23, 1914, United States Department of State, *Foreign Relations of the United States: The Lansing Papers* (2 vols. Washington, 1939), 2, 136–37, 139.

provide expert advisory opinions on delicate questions of neutrality as they arose. The head of the three-man board was James Brown Scott of the Carnegie Endowment for World Peace. Scott and Lansing were similar in temperament, both were trained lawyers, and both sympathized with the British cause—Scott more so than Lansing. Only official position, Scott wrote Lord Bryce, prevented him from saying "how deeply I sympathize with you and your devoted country, and how earnestly I hope that nothing may happen to change its standing in the Society of Nations. But I must not dwell upon this subject if I hope to maintain even the semblance of neutrality."[18] This was the man upon whose views Lansing relied with never a serious sign of disagreement. Thus, significantly, Lansing gave his full approval when Scott, on August 18, 1914, laid down the following principle as a guide for American action: "The burdens of war should bear as lightly as possible upon neutrals, and the rights of neutrals should be as many and their duties as few as is consistent with the observance of neutrality. . . . the Board believes that the United States is entitled to adopt the least burdensome interpretation of its duties of neutrality that is consistent with its traditional policy."[19] Lansing followed this principle and in so doing decided that prohibition by the government of the export of submarine parts was an unnecessarily burdensome interpretation of neutral duties.

A full record of the conversation between Lansing and Schwab's lawyer has not been found, if one was ever made; nevertheless it is possible to reconstruct from the course of events and from Lansing's subsequent opinions what must have been said. Hayden, it appears, told Lansing that there were two ways in which the submarines might be delivered, neither involving the export of completed vessels. First, the finished hulls might

18. Scott to Lord Bryce, October 10, 1914, Bryce MSS, Bodleian Library, Oxford University. This letter has been quoted by Link, *Struggle for Neutrality*, p. 49.

19. Memorandum of August 18, 1914, Department of State file 763.72111/37. The memorandum carries the handwritten notation: "Approved. Robert Lansing."

be shipped, with armament, machinery, etc. sent separately for installation in belligerent territory. Or, second, the hulls might be sent in parts, so that major joining operations would be necessary to finish the submarines. The first and simpler arrangement naturally was preferred by Bethlehem Steel.

Lansing listened and then gave his reasoned reply. He may have pointed out that it was desirable to consult the intent as well as the precise letter of the law. The intent of the American law in this case was to prevent neutral American territory from being used as a base for belligerent naval operations. To ship a completed hull of a submarine, awaiting only the installation of machinery, was close to a violation of the intent of the law. Conceivably the machinery might be installed at sea—just as the *Alabama* received armament in the Azores—and the submarine could commence preying on enemy shipping without ever touching land. In that case, the American port from which the hull was exported would become, in effect, a base of operations against the shipping of a power with which the United States was at peace. Under the obligation to exercise "due diligence," the United States might properly be held responsible by the injured nation. The second procedure, however, was in Lansing's opinion a violation neither of the intent nor of the letter of the law. If the hulls were shipped in parts, the parts would have to be landed in England before they could be assembled. The finished submarines could commence operations only from belligerent territory—not from a neutral port.

Hayden immediately informed Bethlehem Steel of what the Acting Secretary had said, and work on the submarines began on an around-the-clock basis in Bethlehem plants from coast to coast. In Pennsylvania, Bethlehem Steel mills rolled the plate that would be shaped by the shipyards into sections of hull. At the same time the Electric Boat Company, as principal subcontractor, began work on the patented parts and machinery while its subsidiary, the New London Ship and Engine Company, started to build the forty engines required for the twenty submarines. And in Bethlehem's two giant shipyards—the Union Iron Works in San Francisco and the Fore River Shipbuilding Company in Quincy, Massachusetts—workmen gathered and facilities were prepared for the actual construction.

By Monday, November 9, only six days after the Schwab-Fisher meeting, there was so much unusual activity in the Fore River yards that newspaper reporters began asking questions. The next morning the *New York Times* carried on the front page a basically accurate account of the submarine affair. Twenty submarines had been ordered by a belligerent government, the article said, and would be shipped in parts for assembly abroad. Officials of the Company would not name the purchaser, but they did admit that the entire order was worth about $10,000,000.[20] Although this sum was small in comparison to the total orders which Bethlehem received during the war, the value of this one contract equaled 25 per cent of all the orders received by Bethlehem Steel in the calendar year 1913.

On November 10, the day that the *Times* article appeared, Schwab and the Admiralty director of contracts, F. W. Black, signed the formal contract concerning which the two parties had been negotiating for the previous week. Schwab agreed to build twenty submarines according to the specifications used for the H boats for the United States Navy. The boats were to be delivered (at Boston or another East Coast port approved by the Admiralty) "in sections properly packed for shipment." The schedule of delivery called for the

> First four submarines by April 24, 1915 (5½ months)
> Next six submarines by July 10, 1915 (8 months)
> Final ten submarines by September 10, 1915 (10 months)

The Admiralty agreed to pay $500,000 for each boat, subject to a system of bonuses and penalties. For every week in which delivery dates were anticipated, Bethlehem Steel would receive a bonus of £2,000 per boat. If Bethlehem was late in any delivery, it would have to pay £1,000 a week for each late boat. Thus if Schwab could accelerate delivery of all the submarines by five weeks, Bethlehem Steel would receive an additional

20. *New York Times* (November 20, 1914).

£200,000, or nearly $1,000,000. The Admiralty agreed to assume the risks of war and the sea in transporting the parts, but Bethlehem agreed to provide the experts to supervise the assembly of the boats in British territory. The rest of the contract was routine except for the provision that the Admiralty could cancel it, paying Bethlehem costs plus 20 per cent, "in the event of unusual circumstances . . . such as the termination of the present war, *or diplomatic considerations* which made it unnecessary or impracticable to proceed further."[21] The brief allusion to diplomatic considerations is an indication that the Admiralty was not entirely easy over the verbal assurances that Bethlehem Steel had received from Lansing in the Department of State.

To those diplomatic considerations we now turn.

21. Photostatic copy of the contract provided by the Bethlehem Steel Company. Italics added.

4 President Wilson's Intervention

Secretary of State Bryan returned to Washington on Sunday, November 8, just before the story of the submarines broke in the press. Colonel Edward M. House, President Wilson's close adviser and special diplomatic agent, talked to Bryan that afternoon and found him in a highly emotional state of mind. The Secretary spoke violently against military preparedness for the United States and in Colonel House's opinion appeared totally out of touch with reality. "He talked as innocently as my little grandchild," the Colonel wrote in his diary. "I fear he may give trouble."[1] Inwardly, House—like Lansing and James Brown Scott—considered "trouble" to be anything that might work to the disadvantage of Great Britain in the war.

In this mood Bryan challenged Lansing's decision on the submarine contract. Hayden, the Bethlehem lawyer, returned to the Department for further discussion.[2] Reporters, who in those days roamed freely through the corridors of the old State-War-Navy Building in Washington, wrote that an investigation was being conducted and that the company might be required to give up the contract.[3] On the latter point the press was guessing, for a definite decision would not be made by the government for many days. Meanwhile, Lansing care-

1. Diary of Edward M. House, November 8, 1914, House Collection, Yale University Library, New Haven, Connecticut.
2. Lansing desk diary, November 10, 1914.
3. *Wall Street Journal* (November 11, 1914).

fully and patiently told Bryan why the contract as proposed—
shipment of parts and hulls in sections—was no violation of
the law. Bryan refused to be convinced. Lansing repeated himself in writing: a vessel departing from the United States in
condition to conduct offensive operations, or to be prepared for
operations, without entering another port would be in violation of neutrality.

> On the other hand, the sale of material for warships how-
> ever completely prepared for assembling is not the sale of
> a warship or the outfitting of a warship, any more than the
> independent sale of armor plates, steel ribs, guns, shell
> cases, marine engines or other materials for use in naval
> warfare constitute the outfitting of a warship. There is
> nothing unneutral in such shipments. If the parts of a sub-
> marine were shipped in different vessels, certainly no ques-
> tion could be raised, and, if they are all shipped in one
> vessel, I fail to see any difference in principle, so long as a
> port of the purchaser must be reached before the parts can
> be assembled.[4]

Bryan studied the written opinion, conceded that perhaps
Lansing was correct in a narrow technical sense, but still felt
that the contract ought to be stopped. The Secretary sought the
President's opinion and support. He sent Wilson a copy of
Lansing's letter, but remarked, "I fear we would be 'skating
on thin ice' if we adopted the rule stated. . . . I am afraid we
could not convince the average citizen there was any difference
in allowing a vessel to be completed here and allowing the parts
to be made so that a complete vessel could be shipped and the
parts assembled in another port." The Secretary's appeal to the
"average citizen" was, of course, an indirect way of saying that
he could not himself see the difference between selling parts
and selling a whole warship. Bryan ended his letter by urging
caution. "If you are in doubt about the matter I would like

4. Lansing to Bryan, November 12, 1914, Lansing MSS.

to talk to you before the matter is finally settled, as I think there is danger in the proposition."[5]

By "danger" it is unlikely that Bryan meant the possibility that the United States might be held legally responsible by Germany for damage done by the submarines. More probably he was alluding to mounting domestic political pressure on the administration, principally from German-American sources, to curtail or stop the growing export of munitions to the Allies.[6] Congress was to convene in a few weeks, and a failure to stop the now much-publicized submarine contract would provide critics of the administration with dangerously strong evidence to support the charge of unneutrality. Already the German ambassador, Count von Bernstorff, was doing his best to complicate the issue. While refraining from formal protest, he talked freely with the press (as was his practice) and exploited the reports of the submarine contract in an effort to foster the impression "that it was a flagrant breach of neutrality to allow the Allies to get what . . . Germany was unable to get."[7]

Thus by November 12 the battle of opinions within the State Department was clearly drawn: Bryan versus Lansing, intuition versus the letter of the law. An appeal had been made to the President. The President would decide. In the days that followed Lansing marshaled the full weight of precedent behind his position. His procedure provides an excellent example of the application of legal methods to a specific question of foreign policy. His first step was to ask the Joint State and Navy Neutrality Board for an advisory opinion. The Board, on November 25, submitted a twelve-page memorandum in which the legal viewpoint was exhaustively argued. According to the Board there were two questions at issue: (1) When did a vessel

5. Bryan to Wilson, November 12, 1914, Bryan MSS, Diplomatic, Legal, and Fiscal Branch, National Archives, Washington, D.C.

6. On German-American activities in support of a munitions embargo see Clifton James Child, *The German-Americans in Politics, 1914–1917* (Madison, 1939), chap. 3. Also Carl Wittke, *German-Americans and the World War* (Columbus, 1936).

7. *Times* (London), quoting the *New York World* of November 13, 1914; see also the *Wall Street Journal* (November 13, 1914).

become a vessel within the meaning of the neutrality law; and
(2) Was the shipment of a vessel in parts a violation of the law?
On each point the Board was able to cite interesting precedents.[8]

On the first point, the Supreme Court in its decision in the
case of Tucker versus Alexandroff (1902) had given a precise
definition of the moment a vessel was born in the legal sense.
In this case the Russian government had contracted with a
Philadelphia shipbuilding firm (William Cramp and Son) for
the construction of a cruiser, the *Variag*. While the *Variag* was
still on the stocks, the Russian Navy sent an officer and fifty-
three men to Philadelphia to take possession of the vessel upon
its completion. The men were quartered in Philadelphia. While
they waited, the *Variag* was launched, although it remained in
the control of the shipbuilders, who had more work to do before turning the vessel over to its skeleton crew. At this juncture
a Russian sailor, one Leo Alexandroff, deserted. William R.
Tucker, Russian vice-consul in Philadelphia, then sought and
obtained Alexandroff's capture and imprisonment by local law
enforcement officers. The vice-consul acted under article IX of
the Russian-American Treaty of 1832, which gave consuls authorization to obtain the assistance of local officials in imprison-
ing "deserters from ships of war and merchant vessels of their
country."

Alexandroff petitioned for a writ of habeas corpus. His case
was heard by a Federal District Court and then by the Circuit
Court of Appeals. Both Courts declared that Alexandroff's imprisonment was not authorized under the Treaty of 1832, because "the *Variag* was not, at the time petitioner left the service,
a Russian Ship of War, but simply an unfinished vessel intended
for a Russian Cruiser [and] that petitioner had not become a
member of her crew . . . inasmuch as the men assigned to that
duty had not yet begun that service." Vice-consul Tucker, un-
daunted by these decisions, obtained a review of the case by
the Supreme Court, which by a 5–4 decision overturned the

8. Papers of the Joint State and Navy Neutrality Board, No. 50, November 25, 1914, Department of State file 763.72111/7321, Foreign Affairs Branch,
National Archives.

opinions of the lower courts. The majority argued that Alexandroff was a crew member even though he had never boarded the *Variag* and that the *Variag* at the time of the desertion was indeed a ship of war. The key sentences of the Supreme Court bearing on the status of Schwab's submarines are: "A ship is born when she is launched, and lives so long as her identity is preserved. Prior to her launching she is a mere congeries of wood and iron—an ordinary piece of personal property—as distinctly a land structure as a house. . . . In her baptism of launching she receives her name, and from the moment her keel touches the water she is transformed, and becomes a subject of admiralty jurisdiction."[9]

The Joint State and Navy Neutrality Board felt that this case offered considerable guidance, but that circumstances and the novel nature of the submarine required some modification in the legal definition of a vessel. The Board recommended that "for the purpose of avoiding an infraction of this Government's delicate neutrality obligations, the birth of a submarine be regarded as her completion fit for launching, rather than the launching itself." The Board further suggested the issuing of an executive pronouncement declaring that the government would consider the neutrality laws in effect "the moment a submarine built to belligerent order has reached a condition fit for launching, whatever procedure thereafter may be intended by the builders." This opinion, supporting what Lansing had originally said to Schwab's lawyer, meant that the Board considered the shipment of a complete submarine hull to be a violation of the law. This opinion would also rule out a procedure by which a submarine could be completed and then knocked down for shipment in sections.

The Board next considered the second question: Was the shipment of parts of a submarine which had not been brought to the point of launching a violation? Again agreeing with Lansing, the Board answered emphatically in the negative. Again a precedent was found. In the summer of 1879, during

9. 183 U.S. 424.

the war between Chile and Peru, Secretary of State William M. Evarts had been confronted with a situation similar to that now posed by the Schwab submarines. Five large crates containing a torpedo launch, in sections ready for assembly, arrived at Panama City for transhipment en route from New York to Callao, Peru. The captain of the American steamer which was to take the crates on board at Panama City refused to do so, fearing an infraction of American neutrality law. The United States customs inspector on the scene sought an opinion from Washington. Evarts ordered a thorough investigation by the legal officer in the Department of State, conferred with the Secretary of the Treasury and the Chilean minister to the United States, and then gave his opinion. The crated parts were, he said, undoubtedly contraband of war and thus were shipped "at the peril of risk and capture," but their shipment was in no sense a violation of American law. There were no grounds upon which the executive officers of the United States could interfere with the transaction.[10]

The Neutrality Board in 1914 agreed with the soundness of Secretary Evarts' opinion and felt it applied without doubt to the contemplated shipment of submarine parts. Lansing, thus fortified, continued his efforts to change Bryan's mind and to influence President Wilson, who, on this matter, was daily growing more inclined to agree with his Secretary of State. Lansing tried by phone to persuade the President, but Wilson —like Bryan—showed signs of impatience with arguments based on legal technicalities. Finally Lansing sent the President a file of papers on the case, including the twelve-page memorandum from the Joint State and Navy Neutrality Board. Wilson, unmoved, decided the time had come to end discussion. On the last day of November he gave Lansing final instructions. "I feel," wrote the President, "that it is really our duty (in the *spirit* at any rate, of the *Alabama* decision) to prevent submarines being shipped from this country even in parts, and I

10. John Bassett Moore, *A Digest of International Law* (8 vols. Washington, 1906), 7, 960–61.

hope you will find a way of checking and preventing this if it is contemplated."[11] Lansing had lost the contest, and Bryan's intuitive approach had triumphed over legal argument.

Lansing was now faced with an embarrassing duty. He had to inform the Bethlehem Steel Corporation that, notwithstanding his original opinion, the government did not approve of the submarine contract and that the submarines, or parts, must not be exported. By this time considerable progress had been made on them. The United States naval inspector stationed at the Fore River Shipbuilding yard was able to report, for example, that twelve submarines were being built there and the remaining eight at the Union Iron Works in San Francisco.[12] Such reports made Lansing's task no easier, but he grasped the nettle and wrote bluntly to Bethlehem Steel's lawyer in Washington that the President and the Secretary of State felt that the contract was a violation of neutrality. Therefore, "this Government is opposed . . . and . . . will take all legal means to prevent exportation of such craft and manufactured parts."[13]

This letter produced an immediate reaction. More was at stake for Bethlehem Steel than twenty submarines and a ten-million-dollar contract. Schwab's goal was to make Bethlehem the unchallenged leader in the production of munitions for the Allies, and thus to increase as much as possible the advantage Bethlehem held over other companies. In order to achieve this goal, initial performance was all important. Measured against tens and hundreds of millions of dollars in contracts that might be forthcoming in the course of a long war, the contract for submarines was not large, but it was among Bethlehem's first

11. Wilson to Lansing, November 30, 1914, *Foreign Relations of the United States: The Lansing Papers, 1,* 115.

12. Copies of reports from T. G. Roberts, Office of the Superintending Constructor for the U.S. Navy, to the Director of Naval Intelligence, November 17 and December 1, 1914, Department of State file 763.72111/1702. For additional Navy reports on the submarine contract see the Office of Naval Intelligence register number 3749, Record Group 38, Navy Branch, National Archives.

13. Lansing to Hayden, December 1, 1914, *Foreign Relations of the United States, 1914, Supplement, The World War* (Washington, 1928), p. 577.

war contracts, and it was equal to one quarter of a normal peacetime year's business. Schwab had promised to build the submarines with unprecedented speed. If he could live up to his promise, the favorable impression thus created would be of value beyond calculation. Should he fail so early in the war, however, his dreams of Bethlehem's pre-eminence could well be blighted. Realizing these things, Schwab (who had arrived back in the United States on November 20)[14] hurried from New York to Washington. First, in order to convey to the British government his determination to do everything possible to complete the contract, he called at the British Embassy and conferred with Ambassador Sir Cecil Spring-Rice. The two men agreed that Schwab's plans were in conformity with accepted principles of international law. Had not an American manufacturer, Schwab pointed out, exported submarines in parts to a belligerent during the Russo-Japanese War? Indeed, answered Spring-Rice, he had been stationed in St. Petersburg at the time and had a personal recollection of the case. Nevertheless, Schwab told the ambassador, the attitude of the American government now seemed doubtful. He was about to call on the Secretary of State and would let the ambassador know what happened at the interview.[15] Spring-Rice himself was pessimistic because, with Congress scheduled to convene in less than a week, he expected Great Britain to be portrayed in the role of a villain. In a private letter to Sir Edward Grey he told of his fears that the administration, under pressure to avoid the appearance of favoring either side in the war, might modify the existing rules of neutrality to Britain's disadvantage since, owing to British control of the seas, the existing rules were operating to Germany's disadvantage. He did not expect that the export of finished submarine parts would be allowed, but because all discussions were being conducted between Bethlehem and the administra-

14. Schwab returned on the *Adriatic* and immediately denied to reporters that he had received any large war contracts. "I have no orders for the building of submarines," he said. *Wall Street Journal* (November 21, 1914).

15. Spring-Rice to Sir Edward Grey, telegram, December 11, 1914, copy in Borden MSS.

tion, he had refrained from making any official representations on the question.[16]

Schwab went from the Embassy to the State Department, where a conference was held with Bryan, Lansing, Schwab, and various subordinates.[17] Schwab argued so vigorously in behalf of his right to export submarines in parts that Bryan weakened and said he would talk to the President again. But Wilson, having made up his mind, was characteristically rigid in his refusal to reconsider. He told Bryan that Schwab's appeal only served to strengthen his original opinion. Schwab, like many men before and after him, had apparently damaged rather than advanced his cause by trying to change Woodrow Wilson's mind.

Without waiting to hear the President's answer to his appeal, Schwab left Washington on a hurried and supposedly secret trip to Montreal, Canada.[18] He was back in New York on December 4 and from there telephoned Bryan, who reported that the President was adamant in his disapproval. Schwab thereupon turned suddenly compliant and promised that "his firm would not build submarines for any belligerent country for delivery during the war." The day after this phone conversation Schwab was on board the *Lusitania* headed again for England. While Schwab was in mid-Atlantic, Bryan issued by pre-arrangement a public statement which reviewed the Schwab-Bryan discussions in surprising detail and announced Schwab's promise. "This closes the submarine incident," the announcement confidently proclaimed.[19]

Schwab's promise, announced with such obvious satisfaction by Secretary Bryan, produced varied but, on the whole, predictable reactions in the United States and abroad. Bryan displayed relief. He imagined that Schwab's promise had headed off potentially dangerous criticisms of the administration from

16. Spring-Rice to Grey, December 11, 1914, Grey MSS, Foreign Office Library, London.
17. Lansing Desk Diary, December 2, 1914.
18. See below, pp. 78–79.
19. *New York Times* (December 8, 1914).

German-Americans. He happily and quickly cabled a report of his triumph to the American ambassador in Berlin: "You will see that no submarines will be built in the United States for delivery to belligerents during the war. Mr. Schwab's company will not build any and we have heard of no other company that has proposed to do so. The decision in this case will doubtless prevent any further discussion of marine building in this country."[20]

Wilson also derived great satisfaction from the apparent outcome of the affair. He, like Bryan, felt that success against Schwab's submarines was useful in replying to those critics who were pressing hard for a general embargo on the export of munitions. Thus, Wilson wrote immediately to Jacob H. Schiff, prominent financier, philanthropist, and supporter of the arms embargo movement: "In a single recent case I saw my way clear to act. When it came to the manufacture of constituent parts of submarines and their shipment abroad complete, to be put together elsewhere, it seemed to me clearly my privilege, acting in the spirit of the *Alabama* case, to say that the government could not allow that, and the Fore River Ship Building Company which is said to have undertaken the contract has cancelled them."[21] But Wilson, of course, could not please everyone, and the pro-British among his critics were indignant. Senator Henry Cabot Lodge, for example, felt that the submarine affair was but one of many of the President's deeds proving that "in an underhand way" Wilson was trying to help Germany. "He has cut off the French loan; he has prevented Schwab from exporting parts of submarines. He has remained silent in regard to the violation of Belgium's neutrality by Germany." So Lodge complained to Theodore Roosevelt.[22]

Although the administration's intervention against the con-

20. Bryan to James W. Gerard, telegram, December 8, 1914, Department of State file 763.72111/1072.
21. Wilson to Schiff, December 8, 1914, Ray Stannard Baker, *The Life and Letters of Woodrow Wilson* (8 vols. Garden City, 1927–39), 5, 188–89.
22. Lodge to Roosevelt, January 15, 1915, Theodore Roosevelt MSS, Division of Manuscripts, Library of Congress.

tract met the demands of the German-American press, other
newspapers were mixed in their reactions. Some, like the Philadelphia *Public Ledger,* felt that there could be "no possible
doubt in the circumstances" of the administration's decision.
The New York *World* also approved and drew the obvious
parallel between Schwab's submarines and the *Alabama.* But
other papers felt that the loss of this large order was an unnecessary hardship to the workmen who would have gained
employment thereby. The *Brooklyn Eagle,* for example, charged
that Wilson's efforts to maintain the appearance of pure neutrality were excessive. He was "leaning backward" in order to
"stand straight." The *Eagle,* perhaps hoping to appeal to
Wilsonian idealism, added a novel variation to the economic
argument. Everything within the law should be done to increase
trade, the paper said, "in order that depression here may not
make it impossible for us to help the rest of the world in emergency conditions."[23] In London the *Times* called Wilson's
intervention "a distinct score for Germany . . . For some time
past German propagandists have been agitating about the submarine business, they had their way."[24]

Spring-Rice, the British ambassador, reacted with calm toler-
ance (quite remarkable when compared with the almost hys-
terical suspicion of Wilson that he had developed by 1916). The
administration's decision, in Spring-Rice's opinion, was the result solely of domestic political considerations. He reported that
Bryan had told him that "possible excitement in Congress" was
the reason for the public statement.[25] "There is no doubt,"
Spring-Rice wrote in another communication, "that the measure if allowed even in accord with diplomatic precedent would
have excited a good deal of hostile remarks and that the German vote would have been strongly mobilized against it."[26]

Spring-Rice continued to refrain from official representations
on the question, but he did talk at length with Lansing. The

23. *Literary Digest, 49* (December 19, 1914), 1208.
24. December 10, 1914.
25. Spring-Rice to Grey, telegram, December 8, 1914, copy in Fisher MSS.
26. Spring-Rice to Grey, telegram, December 11, 1914, copy in Borden MSS.

conversation dealt more with the general possibility of interference with munitions exports than with the specific submarine issue. If Congress contrived to annul contracts that
were in accord with international law, Spring-Rice pointed out,
the "result to American trade in future might be extremely
detrimental."[27] The over-all impression conveyed by Spring-
Rice was, however, that he half welcomed Wilson's intervention against the submarines as a sop thrown to the embargo
advocates, with the thought that by surrendering the submarines, Britain had preserved the unimpeded flow of ordinary
munitions.

But when the news reached London, there was no welcome in
the Admiralty. When Admiral Lord Fisher read Spring-Rice's
telegram, he flew into a rage. His long crusade for an adequate
number of submarines, which had appeared so marvelously
fulfilled a month before, was now seemingly dashed by the action of the United States Government. On the margin of the
telegram he scrawled, with heavy green pencil: "He that is
not with us is against us! We ought to speak out. We are a poor
lot!" At Buckingham Palace, King George V also read of Wilson's intervention. The King wrote to Fisher: "That is rather a
blow isn't it, what are we going to do?"

What would be done? A message had been received from
Schwab that he was on his way. There was still room for hope.
At least so thought Churchill, who, seeking to sooth his irate
First Sea Lord, advised: "Let us see what Schwab has to say."[28]

What Schwab had to say was all important, but it is essential
first that we examine the reaction in Canada to the apparent
cancelation of the contract.

27. Spring-Rice to Grey, telegram, December 8, 1914, Fisher MSS.
28. Marginal notations by Fisher and Churchill, December 12, 1914, on
copy of Spring-Rice's telegram to Grey of December 8 and on copy of King
George V's letter to Fisher, Fisher MSS.

5 *Prime Minister Borden's Opportunity*

Of all the reactions to the apparent cancelation of Schwab's contract the most important for the subsequent history of the affair took place in Canada. Government officials and industrialists saw a great opportunity about to descend. Canada, it appeared, could step into the breach and do the job which her giant neighbor and rival could not. The Royal Navy would get the urgently needed submarines and Canada would get jobs, profits, and prestige.

Within four days of Bryan's announcement Prime Minister Sir Robert Borden in Ottawa had received offers to build submarines from Canadian companies on both coasts and the Great Lakes. Canadian Vickers, Ltd., in Montreal and the Western Dry Dock Company in Port Arthur both offered to build on a cost-plus-percentage basis, while the Canada Ship Building Company at Niagara offered either to build or to turn their plant over to the British government. From British Columbia Sir Richard McBride—who had already engineered one episode involving submarines—reported that submarines could be completed on the Pacific Coast within ten months.

All this information Borden dispatched by cable to London, in hope that the British Admiralty would award the canceled contract to Canada. Such a happy development would help meet two of the Canadian government's most fervently desired objectives. The first, a result of Canada's involvement in the war, was to secure the greatest possible volume of war orders from Great

Britain and the Allies so that the serious unemployment which had spread across the Dominion since August 1914 might be eased. To capture a contract that had originally gone to the United States would be especially gratifying in terms of Canadian national feeling as well as economic advantage. The second objective, although connected with the first, was more specific and had been pursued long before the outbreak of war. It was to secure the establishment in Canada of a modern naval shipbuilding industry. An understanding of these intertwined objectives is essential as background to the further unfolding of the history of the submarines.

The outbreak of hostilities caused serious economic problems in Canada. Depressed conditions, evident all during 1914, were intensified by the dislocation of war. The Canadian government's first problem in the autumn of 1914 was the preparation of troop contingents for overseas duty, but the second problem was the economy and specifically unemployment.

Hard times seemed particularly intolerable in comparison with the boom which Canada had enjoyed since the turn of the century. For the Canadian economy the twentieth century had opened like a locomotive with the throttle full out. Immigrants by the hundred thousand crossed from Europe and flowed north from the United States. The land echoed to the clang of hammer against railroad spike as heavy capital investment—an estimated $2 billion in railroads alone between 1900 and 1913— poured into the country, principally from England. Wheat, of course, was the driving force behind the boom. The size of the crop quadrupled in the first decade of the century, and in the 1913–14 crop year Canada's wheat exports (142 million bushels) were more than one-fifth of the wheat exports for the world. As noticeable as the prosperity in agriculture was the quickening pace of Canada's industrial development east of the Lakes. From Windsor, opposite Detroit, northeastward to Montreal stretched a widening belt of small towns growing large, and large towns becoming cities. Here hundreds of factories turned out plows and refrigerators, automobiles and freight cars, locomotives and textiles. In the years before the outbreak of war Canada acquired the foundations of a modern industrial society.

In this process of rapid industrial growth the year 1911 was of great political significance. The Liberal party under Prime Minister Sir Wilfrid Laurier, in office since 1896, proposed a reciprocal trade agreement with the United States. The agreement called for free trade in natural products and was designed as a boon to Canada's farmers. Rallying behind Borden the Conservative opposition attacked the reciprocity agreement on patriotic and, above all, economic grounds. Reciprocity, said the Conservatives, would bring Canada under the domination of the United States, weaken her ties with the Empire, and prevent her from growing into a self-sufficient industrial nation. Generously financed by railroad and manufacturing interests, the Conservatives forced a general election and ousted the Liberals. In October 1911 Borden became prime minister. He won primarily because the majority of the Canadian people believed that the rejection of reciprocity was necessary to ensure continued industrial property and development. Furthermore, by ostentatiously turning Canada's back on the United States the Conservatives had both catered to and further stimulated the vague but powerful sense of national identity within the Dominion. Proudly, men spoke of the defeat of reciprocity as a Canadian declaration of independence. Borden, like countless politicians in underdeveloped countries before and since, had discovered that a double appeal to economic interest and popular nationalism was a magic political formula, especially when the young nation faced a real or imagined external threat. During all of the decade in which Borden remained prime minister after the heady victory of 1911 he remained extremely sensitive to the needs of Canadian industry and to the psychological drive to emphasize the Dominion's national identity. His response to these two needs are the twin themes of his decade in office, themes which unify and explain virtually all of his activities.

For two years after the Conservative victory in 1911 the Canadian economy continued prosperous. But in late 1913 and early 1914 something went wrong. Construction was sharply curtailed. The tide of immigration receded. The winter of 1913–14 saw heavy unemployment, and the coming of summer failed to bring the expected improvement. The *Labour Gazette,* the Department of Labour's comprehensive monthly survey, noted in July 1914 that "a number of plants shut down indefinitely and large bodies of men [were] laid off." City by city the picture was bleak. "Employment conditions in Montreal have rarely been worse." Ottawa was enduring "the most discouraging labour situation in years." In Toronto "the number of unemployed was still considerable, including many skilled mechanics." Out in Vancouver the "extent of unemployment was greater than it has ever been at this season of the year."[1]

With the outbreak of war the weak economy fell into a state of near paralysis. The correspondents of the *Labour Gazette* told the story in detail. At Sydney Mines, Nova Scotia, the steel plant "closed down completely and men and officials were paid off." In Toronto "the labour situation entered upon a more serious phase than at any previous time. . . . The British Welcome League [a receiving center for immigrants], recently closed, will be used during the coming season to accommodate the unemployed."[2] From every corner of Canada came similar dark reports.

But in the bleakest days at the beginning of the war a flutter of optimism appeared in Canadian industrial circles. Might not the war provide Canada with an unprecedented commercial opportunity? Before the full horror of the conflict could be grasped, some trade journals indulged in undisguised jubilation. *Industrial Canada* (organ of the influential Canadian Manufacturers' Association), for example, gleefully printed[3] a statistical chart of German trade which Canada could easily

1. *Labour Gazette, 15* (July 1914), 1, 19, 32.
2. Ibid. (September 1914), 339, 359.
3. September 1914.

capture. The chart was headed "Rich Prizes for Canadian Manufacturers." The government encouraged these naïve hopes. The *Weekly Bulletin* of the Department of Trade and Commerce dealt with little else but the coming golden age as Canadian exporters supplanted German merchants in Western Europe, Russia, Latin America, and the Far East.

It did not take many weeks, however, to demonstrate the absurdity of this illusion of a great boom in general trade during the war. At the same time, it occurred to Canadian industrialists and to the government that the one path out of depression and to prosperity was paved with potential orders placed in Canada for war materials. Hopefully, Canadians reasoned that the Dominion, as part of the British Empire, would soon be deluged with orders from Great Britain and her principal allies, France and Russia. Through September and into October, Canada waited. Where were the orders? A small number—for blankets and saddles—were received by the Department of Militia, and in September tentative steps were taken to organize a "Shell Committee" to supervise the production of munitions. But still unemployment mounted. Then the intolerable occurred. Newspapers began to carry accounts of large orders being placed by Great Britain and France in the United States, orders for products which Canadians claimed could be supplied just as quickly and cheaply in Canada.

What was wrong? Perhaps the government had failed to advertise the extent of Canada's resources. Soon complaints and demands for action began coming into Ottawa. Prime Minister Borden read the complaints with concern, decided that the British government needed prodding, and on September 24, 1914, sent a diplomatically worded cable to London. Speaking formally through the Governor-General, Borden said:

> My advisers are informed that supplies of many different articles required for war purposes can be procured in Canada of good quality at reasonable prices. In view of serious conditions of unemployment they would be glad to have Canadian manufacturers and producers considered

as far as practicable. Canadian and United States press continually report that orders for such supplies are being placed in the United States.[4]

In due time the Secretary of State for the Colonies replied from London with vague assurances: "Your Ministers can rely on our bearing in mind the possibilities of Canada as a source of supply for war purposes and on our taking full advantage of them as occasion arises."[5]

This mild exchange of messages appeared to produce no results. November came, and the situation as Borden saw it was grave. Day by day more reports appeared in the press of huge orders being placed in the United States; among them Borden may well have noticed Schwab's much-publicized submarine contract. Meanwhile, the approach of cold weather meant hardship in Canada. The unemployed cried for heavy public expenditures to create jobs, but business stagnation had resulted in a sharp falling off in government tax revenues. Borden—who had a tendency to exaggerate bad news—began to feel that Canada was vibrating with discontent which, if unassuaged, might endanger not only the position of his Conservative party (serious consideration was then being given to the advisability of calling a general election), but also the vigor of the Dominion's war effort, and perhaps even Canada's ties to the Empire. Borden feared that if the economy were not strengthened, and quickly, full Canadian participation in the war might prove impossible to maintain.

Borden decided to send a truly energetic protest, not through the cumbersome machinery of the Colonial Office, where every complaint was muffled and many were lost, but direct to the appropriate British departments via the Canadian High Commissioner in London. The immediate impetus to the protest

4. Governor-General to Colonial Secretary, telegram, September 24, 1914, in A. Fortescue Duguid, *Official History of the Canadian Forces in the Great War 1914–1919*, General Series, Vol. 1, Pt. II (Ottawa, 1938), appendix 168.

5. Ibid., appendix 169.

occurred on November 26. The manufacturers who came to see Borden on that day were particularly bitter in denunciation of British orders going unnecessarily to the United States. For example, the prominent representative of a large wagon firm reported that hundreds of men were out of jobs in his city because the British and French had refused to place orders in Canada. He told Borden that he employed "active agents of first class standing in London" and that he had traveled personally to New York to see the French purchasing commission, but that his efforts had produced only refusals unaccompanied by any explanation. After listening to such tales, Borden's patience came to an end; in a long cable to High Commissioner Sir George Perley in London he used strong words:

> Not only the people of Canada as a whole but individuals are making sacrifices undreamed of to support the Empire in this war. A very painful and even bitter feeling is being aroused throughout the Dominion. Men are going without bread in Canada while those across the line are receiving wages for work that could be done as efficiently and as cheaply in this country. You cannot emphasize too strongly the consideration set forth in this message. Public opinion is being seriously aroused as to most gravely affect our future action.[6]

Thus, at the moment President Wilson was about to decide that the American government could not allow Bethlehem Steel's contract for submarines for the British Navy, Borden believed that Anglo-Canadian relations were at a most critical pass. The situation could be saved only by large and immediate war orders. One type of war order which in Borden's eyes would be particularly welcome was for naval vessels. To understand why this was so and how the eagerness to see the establishment of a naval shipbuilding industry relates to the history of the submarines, it is necessary to go back several years before the outbreak of the Great War.

6. Borden to Perley, telegram, November 27, 1914, Perley MSS.

The coming of the iron ship destroyed the once-proud ship-building industry of Canada. By the beginning of the twentieth century all of the larger vessels under Canadian registry were built abroad, mostly in Great Britain. There was no Canadian Navy and, of course, no naval shipbuilding. Canada, however, was not immune from the influence of worldwide acceleration in naval building with which the century opened, or to that special and intense aspect of the acceleration, the Anglo-German naval rivalry. Inevitably, men began to talk of building warships in Canada.

One of these men was Frederick Orr Lewis, a successful Montreal hardware manufacturer and agent in Canada for Vickers-Maxim & Sons, the huge British armaments and shipbuilding firm. Lewis did more than talk; he founded Canadian Vickers, Ltd., the firm which for years was at the center of every discussion of naval shipbuilding in Canada and in whose yards the submarines of our story were launched.

In 1907 after years of soliciting orders in Canada for execution by Vickers in Great Britain, Lewis took the first steps toward the establishment of a manufacturing subsidiary in Montreal. At the Colonial Conference between the Dominion and United Kingdom governments held in London that year there was much discussion of the role of the colonies in naval defense of the Empire. Some men suggested that the Dominions should help finance the Royal Navy; others argued that the Dominions should maintain navies of their own, thus relieving Britain of burdensome local responsibility while satisfying their own growing national pride. In this latter sentiment Lewis saw his opportunity. If the Canadian government should decide on a separate Canadian Navy (given the strength of national feeling cash contributions seemed most unlikely), ships would have to be built. If the shipbuilding facilities were available in Canada, the government would certainly prefer to spend the people's money at home rather than in Britain.

When Prime Minister Laurier was in London for the Colonial Conference in the spring of 1907 Lewis began actively to promote his project for a Canadian branch of Vickers. The plan

had two phases: first, a plant would be established for the manufacture of locomotives for the rapidly expanding Canadian
railways. By the time this plant was in successful operation the
Canadian government, according to Lewis' calculations, would
be ready to order a navy, and the locomotive project would
then become the forerunner of a shipbuilding yard. The whole
operation, Lewis wrote enthusiastically to Laurier, "will mean
a total investment of more than $10,000,000 of new English
money." Lewis arranged an interview in London between
Laurier, Albert Vickers, and Sir Trevor Dawson, the chairman
and vice chairman of Vickers. Thereafter an investigating party
of seven from Vickers spent nearly two months in Canada looking into Lewis' proposals.[7]

Although prospects appeared bright for a moment, they soon
dimmed. Laurier decided against action of any sort on naval
defense, and the directors of Vickers decided the time was not
ripe to inaugurate operations in Canada. Lewis, however, was
not discouraged. He continued his campaign, and by 1909 found
that the climate had changed in his favor as a result of the great
"naval scare" of that year (during which it was widely believed
that the German Navy would soon be strong enough to wrest
control of the seas from Britain and thus destroy the British
Empire). As a direct result of the scare in Britain the Canadian
House of Commons passed a resolution introduced by Sir George
Foster, a leading Conservative, affirming Canada's responsibility
to aid in the naval defense of the Empire. In the lengthy debates of 1909 the Laurier government indicated a preference for
a Canadian Navy, composed of ships built at home; and at a
special defense conference in London in 1909 the government
asked the Admiralty to recommend the type of ships most suitable. The Admiralty urged the building of cruisers and destroyers, arguing, incidentally, that submarines were unsuitable
for Canada, at least for the present, because of the exceptional
skills required for officers and men in the submarine service.[8]

7. Lewis to Laurier, August 23, 1907, Laurier MSS, Public Archives of
Canada, Ottawa.
8. Tucker, *Naval Service, 1,* 119–20.

Meanwhile the Vickers management, doubtless influenced by signs that the Canadian government would soon seek appropriations for naval construction, warmed to Lewis' proposals. The next year, 1910, the Laurier Naval Aid Bill, calling for the creation of a separate navy with ships built in Canada, passed the Parliament; Albert Vickers visited Canada in June, and shortly thereafter the decision was made to establish Canadian Vickers, Ltd.[9] The company was formally incorporated in 1911 and construction work commenced on the large yard on the eastern outskirts of Montreal along the St. Lawrence River. But again Lewis' ambitions encountered obstacles. Laurier, facing strong opposition from pacifist elements within his own party, engaged in deliberate procrastination. Not until May 1911 did the government ask for bids for naval construction. By then the Dominion was in the throes of the controversy over reciprocity. During the summer none of the several bids were accepted, although it seemed generally understood that Canadian Vickers would win out. Then came the government's defeat in the elections of September 1911.

When the Conservatives came into power, the future of a Canadian Navy and of shipbuilding in Canada was immediately placed in doubt. On the one hand many ultra imperialists within the Conservative party denied that there was any value in a separate navy of small ships; they urged that all Canada's efforts should be devoted to contributing cash for dreadnoughts for Britain. On the other hand, the Conservatives had just won an election by appealing to Canadian national pride and presenting a vision of an expanding industrial society. How could a policy of simple cash outlay be squared with the desire for national self-sufficiency? The answer was not easy, and Borden —who personally was a nationalist before he was an imperialist —played for time. He announced that he would go to England in the summer of 1912 in order to consult the Admiralty and would announce a policy after that. "In so grave and important

9. See the correspondence for June 1910 on microfilm reel 307, Vickers MSS.

a determination," he told the House of Commons, "it is infinitely better to be right than to be in a hurry."[10]

In the interval Borden did not lack advice, much of it contradictory. First, he listened to Canadian Vickers. He had scarcely taken office as prime minister when Lewis arrived in Ottawa to explain the capabilities of the Vickers plant.[11] At the same time, Lewis made a spectacular public announcement that the works would employ 3,000 men and be able to build battleships, or any ship up to 25,000 tons, nearly double the size of any vessel then using the port of Montreal.[12] Borden, impressed, asked Lewis how long it would take to build a first-class battleship in Canada. Lewis went to England, consulted the officers of the parent company, and answered that the completion of a battleship in Canada would take only six months longer than in Britain, provided that various important parts were made in England. Lewis included an appeal that skillfully mingled business with politics and national patriotism: "As a Canadian I feel the bringing of this great concern to Canada will redound very much to the credit of your Administration."[13] In another letter, Sir Trevor Dawson of the parent company urged Borden to make a quick decision, claiming that the expansion of the Montreal Vickers plant into a major shipbuilding yard would be of advantage not only to Canada but strategically to the Empire, because Montreal was virtually immune from water attack.[14]

On the other hand, the most powerful political voices within the Conservative party demanded a contribution for dreadnoughts rather than a policy limited to building ships in Canada. Borden, having no reason to question the orthodox obsession with the dreadnought as the only standard of naval strength, moved closer and closer to the views of the contribu-

10. Canada, *House of Commons Debates,* November 20, 1911.
11. Lewis to Borden, October 20, 1911, Borden MSS.
12. *Montreal Daily Star* (October 19, 1911).
13. Lewis to Borden, December 6, 1911, Borden MSS.
14. Dawson to Borden, December 4, 1911, ibid.

tionists, although not abandoning hope of seeing some warships built in Canada.

A key individual behind the policy of contribution was the immensely wealthy owner of the *Montreal Star,* Sir Hugh Graham, a man whose journalistic and financial support had been a major factor in the defeat of reciprocity and Borden's electoral victory. Graham appointed himself unofficial midwife for a new naval policy and private liaison between Borden and the British government.[15] Traveling to England in the winter of 1912, he arranged an interview with Winston Churchill, the new First Lord of the Admiralty,[16] in order to unfold a plan which reflected the thinking of the imperialist wing of the Canadian Conservative party. The Canadian government, said Graham, would ask the Admiralty how Canada could best aid in the defense of the Empire. The answer would be "by strengthening the Imperial Navy." Whereupon the Canadian government would propose:

> 1st. A contribution of ships to the Imperial Navy, built in England and on condition that they shall be named after Canadian Provinces, that Canadian lads shall be encouraged to enlist for them. . . .
>
> 2nd. That the ships shall be subject to recall upon giving the British Admiralty sufficient notice to enable the Admiralty to replace them.
>
> 3rd. Canada to have a voice in deliberations from time to time as to control and disposal of the fleet in peace and in war.

According to Graham, Churchill listened to the plan and then cried out: "This is magnificent. If it were made public at a very

15. See the telegram from the Governor-General (the Duke of Connaught) to the Colonial Secretary (Lewis Harcourt), October 24, 1911, Sir Edward Grey MSS. Connaught reported that Graham was in close consultation with Borden and that Graham's proposals could be considered as a "ballon d'essai."

16. Churchill became First Lord on October 25, 1911.

early date it would simply bring the Germans to time. It fills
me with hope. . . . The question is can it be done and done
soon."[17]

Borden also found the Graham formulation congenial as far
as it went. The idea of dreadnoughts with Canadian names and
Canadians among the crews had a sentimental appeal to national pride; the provision that the ships might someday be
recalled left the door open for the eventual establishment of a
separate Canadian Navy; and the insistence on Canadian participation in decisions regarding the use of the fleet—in other
words, foreign policy—was one of Borden's own oft-repeated
demands. But the Graham plan was incomplete. It neglected
Canadian economic interests.

When Borden arrived in England in July 1912 to consult
with the Admiralty, he had virtually made up his mind to propose a contribution for dreadnoughts, with a simultaneous arrangement to encourage shipbuilding in Canada. The Canadian
prime minister's thoughts are revealed by a list of topics for
discussion which he jotted down just before his first conference
with Churchill. The first item was shipbuilding in Canada—
at Montreal and also at Halifax, Borden's own constituency.
The list also contained other items of direct benefit to Canada,
such as dockyards and subsidized steamships. Of particular importance was an item dealing with representation for Canada
on the Committee of Imperial Defence.[18] Borden reasoned that
if Canada was to assume part of the burden of defense, she
must also have a voice in the decisions of foreign policy that
might decide issues of peace and war. This matter of a voice
and the recognition of national status that it would entail runs
like a refrain through all of Borden's dealings with the British
government. It is impossible to place his efforts to promote
Canada's concrete economic interests in one tight compartment
and his drive for recognition of abstract political status in an-

17. Long memorandum by Graham describing his interview with Churchill—undated, but internal evidence suggests December 1911 or early January 1912. Borden MSS.
18. Memorandum in Borden's handwriting, ibid.

other. The two proceeded side by side and were equally a part
of Borden's nationalism.

Borden's mission lasted two months. He attended meetings of
the Committee of Imperial Defence, where he asked a few questions and listened attentively while Sir Edward Grey, Churchill,
and others described the German threat to British security. He
was endlessly advised by politicians, journalists, and admirals.
He watched a Spithead review of the fleet from the Admiralty
yacht *Enchantress*. He knelt before the King at Buckingham
Palace and was sworn in as a Privy Councillor. He spent several
days in Paris in a gesture intended to please Quebec sentiment.[19]

The principal result of this hectic activity was a pair of official memoranda from the Admiralty—one secret, the other
to be made public—on which Borden could base his claim that
an emergency required a Canadian contribution and that time
was too short to allow for the delay required to build dreadnoughts in Canada.

In the rush Borden did not succeed, before his return to
Ottawa, in securing a definite commitment from the Admiralty
on the question of shipbuilding in Canada. But such a commitment was essential; without it Borden feared Parliament might
not vote the contribution. Meanwhile, Canadian Vickers did
not let Borden forget "the splendid progress that has been
made on the site of our Naval Works."[20] Accordingly, Borden
by letter and cable continued to press Churchill for a promise
of building in Canada. Skillfully he argued from broad imperial
lines rather than narrow national positions. "I do not suggest
this in any spirit of bargaining," he wrote, "but you, of course,
realize that conditions of a somewhat difficult character from a
political standpoint will have to be encountered." A failure to
carry the proposed contribution through Parliament would have
a disastrous moral effect upon the whole Empire. "Thus . . .
everything should be done to overcome local prejudice" against
spending Canadian money in England. Specifically, Borden

19. Henry Borden, ed., *Robert Laird Borden: His Memoirs* (2 vols. Toronto, 1938), *1*, 360.
20. F. Orr Lewis to Borden, September 12, 1912, Borden MSS.

urged that destroyers or small cruisers might be built within a very early period in Canada, and that possibly an arrangement might be made to divide the extra cost between the two governments.[21]

Borden's demand—and demand is not too strong a word— put Churchill in a difficult position. The heavy increases in naval expenditure were most distasteful to a large segment of the Cabinet. Churchill knew he would have to fight for every pound. He would have to convince his critics that the Admiralty was practicing every possible economy consistent with the nation's security. How then could he justify the additional cost of building ships in Canada even if the Canadian government did offer to bear part of the extra charges? Furthermore, were the small ships—the destroyers and cruisers—which Borden wished built in Canada necessary, if the dreadnought was the single standard of naval strength? At this time, in the autumn of 1912, Churchill had not yet been won over to Lord Fisher's claim that the days of the dreadnought were numbered. Indeed, as we have seen, Fisher himself was, in spite of his growing enthusiasm for the submarine, toying with the idea of a super-dreadnought to be built in Canada.[22]

Faced with this problem, Churchill tried procrastination, but Borden continued to press for an answer in message after message. On October 26 he urged a quick and definite reply before the imminent opening of Parliament; six days later he pointedly reminded Churchill that no answer had yet been received.[23] Borden also sent, "as an example of the weight which is attached to the expenditure in Canada of the proposed contribution," a resolution passed by the municipal council of the Montreal subdivision in which the Canadian Vickers yard was located. The council pledged its support to a contribution for

21. Borden to Churchill, October 3 and October 5, 1912, copies in Asquith MSS.

22. See above, pp. 16–17 n.

23. Governor-General to the Colonial Secretary ("Following from Prime Minister to the First Lord of the Admiralty"), telegrams, October 26 and November 2, 1912, Asquith MSS.

the naval defense of the Empire provided that "the amount to be contributed be expended within Canada, so that the labouring classes of this country may receive the full benefit thereof."[24]

Under this bombardment Churchill gave Borden a very qualified affirmative answer on November 4, and two days later the Cabinet formally agreed that some work should be given to the Canadian yards.[25] Borden had won his point. Would it be desirable to put the agreement "in official and publishable form," Borden asked, or would Churchill prefer "a discreet statement?"[26] A discreet statement, if you please, Churchill answered.[27] Thus when Borden presented the House of Commons with the call for a cash contribution of $35,000,000 to build three dreadnoughts in Great Britain, he was careful to stress his agreement with the Admiralty. Optimistically, he predicted that a present stimulus to shipbuilding would make it possible in the future to build all vessels required by the government in Canada. "In connection with the development of shipbuilding I should not be surprised to see the establishment of a higher class of engineering works, which would produce articles now imported and not presently manufactured in Canada." Although Canada will spend $35,000,000 in Great Britain, the Admiralty agreement means a "very marked development of more than one industry in Canada . . . even from a purely economic and material standpoint, the step has much to commend it."[28]

Borden was deluged with praise and congratulations for his naval program. To all appearances he had wrought a great triumph for himself, his party, Canada, and the Empire. The praise from England was especially welcome, for it indicated to Borden that he had achieved the double goal of being a suc-

24. Borden to Churchill, November 2, 1912, ibid.

25. Churchill to Borden, telegram, November 4, 1912; and Asquith to King George V, November 6, 1912, ibid.

26. Governor-General to the Colonial Secretary, telegram, November 14, 1912, ibid.

27. Colonial Secretary to the Governor-General, telegram, November 15, 1912, ibid.

28. Canada, *House of Commons Debates,* December 5, 1912.

cessful Canadian and an imperial statesman. Service to nation and service to Empire were identical. "You have no idea what a popular person you are with the ordinary British working man," wrote L. S. Amery from England. "There is no name that gets more rousing cheers the moment it is mentioned than yours. . . . You have somehow caught the imagination of the man in the street."[29] Many felt that the Canadian gesture would not only strengthen the naval defenses of the Empire but so discourage Germany that she would abandon naval rivalry altogether.[30] Borden was thus in a mood of happy exaltation as he looked forward to the quick passage of his program by Parliament. The Empire would be stronger; Canada—having contributed to defense—would soon acquire a voice in the formulation of imperial foreign policy; and under the agreement with Churchill a new naval shipbuilding industry would soon be established in the Dominion.

But the heady mood of December 1912 did not last. Unexpectedly bitter opposition to Borden's program appeared both in Parliament and in the country. Liberals and French Canadians of both political parties denied that the Empire was in danger, refused to believe that Germany had aggressive intentions, and blamed the naval race on a conspiracy of the armaments manufacturers. Canada was in danger of being sucked (in Sir Wilfrid Laurier's famous phrase) into the "vortex of European militarism."

By invoking drastic and seldom-used tactics to close off debate, Borden was finally able to force his bill through the House of Commons in March 1913. The obstacle of the Senate, however, proved insurmountable. With members appointed for life, the Senate was controlled by the Liberals, thanks to that party's long ascendancy (1896–1911). Normally the Senate was an attic for aged politicians who perfunctorily passed all legislation received from the House. But on this occasion—one of the most dramatic and controversial in Canadian political history—the

29. Amery to Borden, December 14, 1912, Borden MSS.
30. Walter Long to Borden, December 24, 1912, ibid.

Senate exercised its almost forgotten constitutional prerogative to thwart the will of the House of Commons. In May 1913 the Naval bill was defeated. "I do not believe there is any chapter in Canadian history quite so humiliating and discreditable as that through which we are passing," wrote a Canadian journalist of imperialist persuasion.[31]

Borden's dream was collapsing. Desperately he groped for an expedient to circumvent the despised Senate. In a cable to Churchill he urged that the British government begin the construction of the three dreadnoughts, on the expectation that Canada would be able to pay for the ships before they were completed. Borden hoped that while the ships were building, normal attrition by death and resignation in the Senate would enable the Conservative party to gain control of that body and thus pass the necessary appropriations.[32] Churchill brought Borden's proposal before the Cabinet, and the Cabinet unanimously turned it down, on the grounds that the arrangement would be attacked "as seeming to go behind the formal decision of the Canadian Parliament and that we have no right to assume that Senate's vote could be reversed."[33] The suggestion, wrote Prime Minister Asquith to the King, "would be in the nature of a gambling transaction and would be construed in Canada as a direct intervention by the Imperial Government in her party controversies." Churchill, who had been counting on the Canadian dreadnoughts, then persuaded the Cabinet "after much discussion," to authorize the acceleration of three British battleships which ordinarily would not have been begun until the spring of 1914.[34]

If Borden's proposal was of dubious wisdom, Churchill's counter suggestion for Canadian action was worse. It was that Borden communicate secretly with "the great contracting firms

31. Sir John Willison to Edward Grigg, May 6, 1913, quoted in *The History of* THE TIMES, Vol. 4, Pt. I (London, 1952), 32–33.
32. Borden to Churchill, telegram, June 2, 1913, Borden MSS.
33. Churchill to Borden, telegram, June 4, 1913, ibid. See also Asquith to the King, June 5, 1913, Asquith MSS.
34. E. L. Woodward, *Great Britain and the German Navy*, p. 413.

like Vickers and Armstrongs" and urge them to build three dreadnoughts "as a speculation" on the understanding that Canada would eventually be able to pay for them.

> The risk of their being left with the ships on their hands would not be a very great one even if by misadventure the policy and intention of the Canadian Government was changed; because if the ships were built or in an advanced stage of construction, the British Government simply could not allow them to pass into any other hands but ours or yours. The danger of having these great weapons loose in the World would be so compulsive that we should be forced, not as a matter of agreement or contract, but by the pressure of events, to take them over ourselves.

Churchill urged the utmost haste for two reasons, neither of them sound or convincing. First, changes in naval technology might require that the Admiralty shift the emphasis of new construction away from dreadnoughts in a few years. If Canada had not acted before this shift took place, it might prove politically embarrassing for Borden to go on urging dreadnoughts when the Admiralty had ceased to recommend them. Although Churchill did not specifically mention undersea warfare, his warning to Borden was obviously a reflection of the crusade conducted by Lord Fisher for more submarines. Build dreadnoughts now, Churchill was saying, for tomorrow they may be obsolete. Churchill also urged haste in order that the Canadian ships might be begun before the beginning of a "naval holiday" he was then attempting to arrange with Germany.

> If Canada had only been able to come in *now* with her 3 ships, I am convinced that we should have got into a position where the Germans would be very glad to have made a clear-cut bargain of a limited character. Convince them by facts that it is useless for them to continue the rivalry and then make it well worth while by a good, fair agreement, to pull up.

Churchill felt it was not too late for Canada to convince Germany.[35]

Borden was no more receptive to Churchill's idea than the British Cabinet had been to the suggestion that they gamble on the dreadnoughts. Thus nothing was done. In the Parliamentary session of 1914 Borden found himself still facing a hostile Senate. He did not reintroduce his naval program.

Churchill, meanwhile, was encountering stiff opposition within the Cabinet about the high level of naval expenditure. In January 1914 a Cabinet crisis occurred; Lloyd George, the Chancellor of the Exchequer, led an attack on Churchill's estimates and demanded a reduction in the number of new dreadnoughts. Churchill, using every conceivable argument to defend himself, significantly placed great emphasis on the position of Canada. If Britain reduced her dreadnought program, he told the Cabinet, Borden would be discredited before the Canadian people. They would charge that the much publicized emergency upon which Borden had justified his request for a contribution in 1912–13 was fraudulent. Not only would Borden be politically betrayed, but the whole future relationship of Canada to the Empire would be placed in jeopardy. Churchill narrowly won the day. Britain continued the frantic pace of the armaments race, devoting the major portion of naval expenditures to the dreadnought.[36] Thus an indirect result of Borden's naval policy, even in failure, was to impede a possible relaxation of the Anglo-German naval rivalry and hinder a shift away from the potentially obsolete dreadnought.

These unfortunate repercussions, evident in historical perspective, were not grasped by Borden. Rather he appears to have grown weary of the whole affair during 1914. The political opposition, on the other hand, took pleasure in taunting Borden for his allegedly bogus emergency. "The atmosphere is pure; the sky is clear," said Sir Wilfrid Laurier as Parliament opened in January 1914. There is no German peril, he added; the only

35. Churchill to Borden, June 30, 1913, Borden MSS.
36. For a succinct account of the crisis of January 1914 see Arthur J. Marder's *The Road to War*, pp. 317-27.

peril is economic depression and unemployment. Laurier then moved that the House censure the government for having failed to do more for the unemployed.[37]

All this time the Canadian Vickers company—founded with such high expectations—stood idle. Because Borden was unable to supply the money for the building of dreadnoughts in Great Britain, the Admiralty made no move to place orders for smaller classes of vessels in Canada. P. L. Miller, the general manager of the company, reported gloomily in March 1914 that ship-building circles in England were adopting a most derisory tone when speaking of shipbuilding in Canada. Unless something concrete was accomplished, said Miller, skilled shipbuilding workers could not be attracted to Canada; nor would other companies consider establishing branches in Canada. "There is not the slightest doubt that our venture here is being critically watched and that a year's idleness on our part would most certainly discourage any similar enterprise on the part of any other large firm." Miller therefore urged the government to give Canadian Vickers the contract for a large icebreaker which it was about to order. "It seems to me that the building of such a ship as this icebreaker . . . in Canada would once and for all put a stop to all such idle statements as I heard in England, and would show that we are not only in earnest in what we are trying to do but that we can do it."[38] Miller's argument was convincing. The contract for the icebreaker was placed with Canadian Vickers, and construction began shortly before the outbreak of war. Subsequently, this icebreaker—named the *J. D. Hazen,* after the Minister of Naval Service—was to play a prominent part in the history of the clandestine submarines.

One more episode which took place before the outbreak of war needs to be recounted. In March 1914 Churchill began to reflect upon the manner in which the flexibility of British naval building was hindered by the commitment to Borden concerning the need for dreadnoughts above all else. "Time is

37. Canada, *House of Commons Debates,* January 19, 1914.
38. P. L. Miller to J. D. Hazen, March 5, 1914, Borden MSS.

passing and naval science is developing," he wrote to Borden in March 1914. "The dangers to which the capital ship is exposed increase continually." Accordingly, Churchill proposed that the Second Sea Lord, Sir John Jellicoe, visit Canada in order to recommend a revised Canadian program.[39] An indication of Borden's waning interest in naval policy is the fact that he did not answer Churchill's suggestion. More than four months elapsed. Finally in July Churchill renewed his suggestion to Sir George Perley, who had just arrived in London as Canadian High Commissioner. Without enthusiasm Borden agreed to receive Jellicoe, and it was arranged that the Admiral would sail for Canada on September 11.[40] War, of course, intervened. Jellicoe did ultimately visit Canada to advise on naval policy, but not until 1919.

To summarize: Borden's dream of a naval shipbuilding industry as part of a policy of defense cooperation with Great Britain had in the three years risen to the optimistic heights of December 1912 and then declined steadily to the summer of 1914. On the eve of war, while waiting apathetically for Jellicoe, he put all thoughts of naval affairs from his mind and went on vacation.

The coming of war created a radically different situation. To the problem of unemployment, discussed in the first part of this chapter, was added the fact that Canada was suddenly contributing more in men and dollars than was ever envisioned in a peacetime naval aid program. These factors revived, and added urgency to, Borden's interest in securing shipbuilding orders for Canada. The two elements in the Canadian background to the history of the clandestine submarines merged: the deep-rooted interest in naval shipbuilding and the more specific and painful necessity of relieving unemployment.

For the first two months of the war the Canadian govern-

39. Churchill to Borden, telegram, March 6, 1914, Perley MSS.
40. Borden to Churchill, telegram, July 23, 1914, ibid.

ment was primarily occupied in raising, equipping, and sending off the first contingent of 33,000 soldiers to England. But early in October, after the troop ships had departed, Borden instructed Perley in London to remind the Admiralty of the unused shipbuilding facilities in Canada and of the Dominion's readiness to contribute to the naval defense of the Empire. Perley went to the Admiralty and was brusquely informed that Canada should confine her assistance in the war to providing men for the Army. The Admiralty said it was impossible for Canada to do "anything effectual" by way of supplying warships—"ships take too long to build."[41]

In the face of this rebuff, Borden temporarily turned his attention to educating the British government in general and the War Office in particular concerning Canada's economic resources. In the first two months of the war Canada did, however, supply one vessel for the war—an icebreaker, which went not to Britain but to Russia. The story of the icebreaker needs to be told, because it relates directly to the submarines, and incidentally illustrates how widely separated and apparently unconnected events may influence each other.

Upon the outbreak of war the Russian government became deeply worried over the inadequacy of the ocean port facilities available for contact with her western allies. Germany controlled the Baltic; the Dardanelles were closed. In Europe only Archangel remained. Under normal conditions Archangel was frozen over for six months of the year. Icebreakers, however, could chip a few precious weeks from each end of the icebound season. Every added day of navigation would mean a Russia made stronger with desperately needed supplies. The success or failure of the Russian armies might ultimately depend upon how well icebreakers in Archangel could perform their task. Russia's problem was where to find more of them. None could be built in time to go into service before the fall freeze. A completed icebreaker would have to be purchased. Where?

The Russian government thought of Canada and in the

41. Perley to Borden, telegram, October 8, 1914, ibid.

middle of August approached Canadian High Commissioner Perley in London, who immediately reported to Ottawa.[42] Borden's first response was negative. Canada, he feared, could be of no assistance.[43] She was already short of icebreakers and was even then awaiting delivery of a new one from Canadian Vickers. The next day, however, Borden asked Perley what specifications the Russians required for the vessel they sought.[44] It took Perley a week to get precise specifications from the Russians and send the information back to Ottawa. Russia needed a very large vessel, one capable of dealing with fifteen to twenty feet of rafted ice and five to six feet of solid ice.[45] There was only one icebreaker in Canada which met these requirements: the *Earl Grey,* a huge new vessel recently built in England and used to maintain winter service between Prince Edward Island and the mainland. Reluctantly, on September 1, Borden cabled that the *Earl Grey* could not be spared.[46]

The Russian government, however, was not to be denied. The commercial attaché in the Embassy in Washington was ordered to Ottawa to argue Russia's need. Within hours of his arrival he gained the Canadian government's agreement to sell the *Earl Grey* for £100,000.[47] When, after some procrastination, the Russian government delivered the cash, the *Earl Grey* sailed for Archangel on October 7.[48] A factor in Ottawa's decision to give up the ship was the excellent progress that Canadian Vickers was making on the icebreaker *J. D. Hazen.* The departure of the *Earl Grey* made speed on the *Hazen* doubly important.

Canadian Vickers, however, was employing only a relative handful of men on the *Hazen* (and a dredger also ordered by the Canadian government). Tentatively the government ap-

42. Ibid., telegram, August 17, 1914, Borden MSS.
43. Borden to Perley, telegram, August 19, 1914, ibid.
44. Ibid., telegram, August 20, 1914, ibid.
45. Perley to Borden, telegram, August 27, 1914, ibid.
46. Borden to Perley, telegram, September 1, 1914, ibid.
47. Governor-General to Colonial Secretary, telegram, September 9, 1914, ibid.
48. Ibid., telegram, October 19, 1914, ibid.

proached the company about building a large number of sub-marines, destroyers, and light cruisers for Canada[49] (since the Admiralty had refused so categorically to consider placing orders). The company readily quoted prices, but the figures were so high, so far above the cost of the same vessels built in England, that Ottawa lost interest.

F. Orr Lewis, president of Canadian Vickers, used every possible appeal to national pride in an effort to win approval from Ottawa. Think of the far-reaching effect the construction of these vessels would have on allied trades throughout the Dominion, he wrote to Hazen. We hope our plant "is destined to be the greatest plant of its kind in North America." In another letter he wrote that the cost would not exceed 50 cents per capita per year. "Looking at it from this standpoint it would not be a very great sacrifice for we Canadians to make at the present time. In fact, taking into consideration the huge sums of money which have been spent throughout the world . . . this would enable Canada to enter into competition at a mere bagatelle in comparison with that expended by any other country or colony."[50] Lewis' eloquence did not succeed. Borden and his colleagues were eager to see the creation of a new industry, but not eager enough to commit large amounts of the government's own money—especially at a time of extraordinary war expenses. Furthermore, by authorizing the construction of a fleet of submarines, destroyers, and cruisers Ottawa would in effect be committing Canada to a separate Navy. This was a fundamental decision that Borden was not yet ready to make. In the autumn of 1914 he was still uncertain how far or how fast he wished to emphasize the independent nationhood of Canada as distinct from nationhood within the Empire.

The reluctance to spend Canada's own money or create a separate Canadian Navy explains the enthusiasm with which Borden greeted the newspaper reports of the apparent cancelation of the Schwab contract for submarines for the Ad-

49. See the correspondence between F. Orr Lewis and Hazen and Lewis and Borden through October and November in the Borden MSS.
50. Lewis to Hazen, November 14, 1914, ibid.

miralty. Here, at last, after years of disappointment was Canada's opportunity. Borden hastened to remind the Admiralty again of Canada's facilities, and to say that Canadian firms could readily supply the submarines.[51] But his messages, through High Commissioner Perley, were completely ignored. To understand why this was so, we must turn our attention again to the activities of Charles M. Schwab.

51. Borden to Perley, telegram, December 11, 1914, ibid.

6 Subterfuge

Charles Schwab's sudden acceptance of the administration's demand that he cancel his contract for submarines was, on the surface, quite uncharacteristic. Why should a man famed for his determination to surmount any obstacle give in so easily? Legally his case was strong. Was not the success of the contract worth a fight? The answer to this puzzle is to be found in Schwab's activities in the short interval between his confrontation with Bryan, December 2, and his apparent acquiescence, December 4, in the administration's demand that the contract be abandoned.

It will be recalled that Bryan, unwilling to take full responsibility for replying to Schwab's entreaties with a categorical negative, had promised to consult President Wilson once again. Schwab, however, harbored no illusions that the president was likely to change his mind, for even as Schwab spoke with Bryan the first outlines of an alternative plan, an ingenious means of circumventing the president, were taking shape in his mind.

Immediate action was required to convert the plan into reality. Every hour gained was vital, for delay in the completion of the contract was almost as serious for the prestige of Bethlehem Steel as cancelation. Schwab therefore went directly from his interview with Bryan to the Washington railroad station and entrained for Montreal. Through the night of December 2 he headed north. By early morning he was in Montreal. His mission was supposed to be secret, but, as usual, newspaper reporters quickly discovered and wrote of his presence in Canada, lacing their stories with rumors some of which came close to the truth. The *New York Times,* for example, reported that Schwab's arrival in Montreal gave rise to the rumor that Bethlehem Steel contemplated building submarines in Canada for Great Britain.[1] The rumor was correct.

The specific purpose of Schwab's trip to Montreal was to inspect the facilities of the Canadian Vickers plant and to confer with P. L. Miller, the general manager. Schwab was accompanied by the chief engineer of the Fore River Shipbuilding Company and two other associates. They went immediately from the railroad station to the shipyard on the outskirts of the city, looked at the huge building sheds and the well-protected launching basin, noted the work in progress, including the icebreaker for the Canadian government, and then departed as swiftly as they had arrived. Their stay in Montreal had been a matter of hours.[2]

Schwab was pleased with what he saw at Canadian Vickers. His tentative plan for escaping the intervention of the Wilson administration in his submarine contract began to take on concrete detail. Although final arrangements could not be made without approval of the Admiralty and of Vickers, Ltd., the parent company in England, Schwab was now confident of ultimate success. As his train headed south into the United States, he decided that he could safely give Secretary of State Bryan the promise that President Wilson wished. Thus when Schwab again reached New York, on December 4, he telephoned Bryan, learned as expected that President Wilson's attitude was unchanged, and then gave the formal promise, on the basis of which Bryan declared that the submarine incident was closed.

Even if Bryan thought the affair was over, the press did not and watched eagerly for the next move. On December 5 Schwab sailed on the *Lusitania* for England—his second trip in six weeks—and a pre-arranged interview with Admiral Lord Fisher

1. *New York Times* (December 5, 1914).
2. Executive Committee Minutes, Canadian Vickers, Ltd., December 7, 1914, Canadian Vickers MSS, Montreal.

and Churchill. The *Wall Street Journal* noted the sudden trip and commented that "steel circles" believed "a way will be found to enable Bethlehem to carry out its submarine contract in conformity with the neutrality laws. Mr. Schwab will be back from Europe in about three weeks."[3] Meanwhile in Montreal interest in the affair was mounting (although in Ottawa Prime Minister Borden was totally unaware that Canada was becoming involved). Officials of Canadian Vickers, quizzed by the press, were tight-lipped. "No statement of the outcome of the negotiations between Charles M. Schwab and the Canadian Vickers Company," commented the *Montreal Daily Star,* "is expected until Mr. Schwab's arrival in England."[4]

While pro-British and anti-administration circles were venting their anger against the president for his intervention, curious reports on the submarine affair were received in Washington by the Director of Naval Intelligence and passed on to the Department of State. If Schwab's contract had been canceled, one would expect the work on the submarines to stop. But this was not the case. From Groton, Connecticut, came a confidential report from a Navy inspector of machinery that the New London Ship and Engine Company was working twenty-four hours a day on forty engines for English submarines. From the Fore River plant the Navy's superintending constructor reported continuing activity but along a mysterious pattern. The work of erecting the submarines upon the stocks had stopped. The keels, previously laid, had been dismantled, and were being shipped elsewhere in parts. Where they were being shipped the superintending constructor did not know. Within the yard's machine shops work was progressing without interruption on various submarine parts.[5] Had the Navy's agents been privy

3. *Wall Street Journal* (December 7, 1914).

4. *Montreal Daily Star* (December 8, 1914).

5. See the copies of letters, both dated December 10, 1914, from the Inspector of Machinery at Groton and the Superintending Constructor for the Navy at the Fore River plant to the Director of Naval Intelligence, Department of State file 763.72111/1746, Diplomatic, Legal, and Fiscal Branch, National Archives.

to the discussions about to take place between Schwab and the Admiralty there would have been no mystery.

At the Admiralty Schwab and Fisher reviewed the new situation created by President Wilson. Schwab, who customarily radiated exuberant optimism, was able to point out that all was not lost. If the Admiralty could arrange for Bethlehem Steel to have unrestricted use of the Canadian Vickers plant, Schwab could build some or all of the submarines in Montreal from parts and materials imported from the Bethlehem plants in the United States. Very little time would be lost. Fisher was immediately persuaded of the soundness of the scheme and quickly the details of a supplementary contract were negotiated. Since the Montreal plant could not accommodate more than ten submarines at one time, it was decided that ten would be built there immediately and that work would proceed on the remaining ten in the United States but with their ultimate form of delivery left open because of the "diplomatic situation." Although the Admiralty agreed to pay the rent for the yard as well as a portion "of the salaries of the Head officers of the establishment at Montreal," and to refund to Bethlehem any duties paid on material imported into Canada, Schwab contended that his costs for completing the vessels under the new arrangement would be substantially higher than for doing all the work in the United States. Accordingly the Admiralty agreed to a basic price of $600,000 for each of the ten Canadian boats instead of $500,000 per submarine as in the original contract; however, the bonus and penalty scale was cut in half, to £1,000 bonus and £500 penalty per submarine per week for early or late delivery. The schedule for delivery called for the completion of the first two Canadian submarines by August 31, 1915, and two each at the end of September, October, November and December.[6] By comparing the revised contract with the original, we see that Schwab had succeeded in raising the price by 20 per cent and extending the delivery dates by several months. Under

6. "Supplementary Heads of Agreement Dated 10th November 1914, December 15, 1914," photostatic copy from Bethlehem Steel Company Archives.

the original contract, it will be recalled, the first four submarines were to be delivered in April and six more in July.
Since the advantage of the greatly extended delivery schedule
was only partially offset by the reduced bonus rate, and since
the Admiralty agreed to pay an additional $100,000 for each
submarine plus all Canadian import duties, Schwab was in a
position to clear a greater profit by assembling the submarines
in Montreal than by having to adhere to the original contract.
Ironically, one of the unintended results of Wilson's intervention was materially to help Bethlehem Steel increase its net
earnings (which rose 157 per cent from 1914 to 1915, from
$9,649,667 to $24,821,408).

Having put his plan into operation, Schwab caught the
Lusitania on its next westward voyage and was back in New
York on December 23. As always, reporters met him at the
gangway and asked why he had gone to England. His statement,
obviously designed to divert attention from the Canadian subterfuge, deserves to be quoted at length if only as a catalog of
deliberate inaccuracy:

> I was in London only two days, and that for the purpose
> of relinquishing several governmental contracts for the
> building of submarines which I had obtained on a previous
> visit to Europe.
>
> I was in doubt as to the status under the neutrality
> declaration of any American shipbuilding company in
> executing orders for submarines or other war vessels for
> belligerent governments.
>
> Accordingly I went to Washington to consult with the
> authorities after obtaining these contracts. After several
> consultations with Secretary Bryan . . . I was shown a law
> passed after the settlement of the Alabama claim to the
> effect that any ships in whole or in sections designed for
> belligerent countries could not be shipped from neutral
> countries without incurring a breach of neutrality.
>
> Secretary Bryan assured me that it was against the spirit
> and letter of the law for me to endeavor to execute any

such contract, and accordingly there was nothing left for me to do but go back to Europe and cancel the contract.

That was the principal part of my business abroad.[7]

While Schwab was publicly declaring that the submarine contract had been canceled, his agents were making arrangements to begin operations in Montreal. Throughout December, Bethlehem engineers and executives arrived at Canadian Vickers. On December 21 the Executive Committee of the Canadian company discussed the necessity of maintaining absolute secrecy in all matters connected with the submarines. A week later, after the arrival of more Fore River officials, the company learned that work on the Canadian government's icebreaker "would have to cease due to lack of equipment." Nothing was to stand in the way of the submarines. The Executive Committee, in its last meeting for the year 1914, learned that the plant was "on loan to the British Admiralty not to the Fore River Company" as had been assumed; that the plant would be taken over from January 1, 1915; and that the vice-president of the Union Iron Works would arrive from San Francisco on January 4 to take complete charge. With the first of the new year materials and skilled specialists began to arrive by rail from the United States. The first keel was laid January 11.[8] In order to camouflage the heavy flow of material from Bethlehem plants into Canada, the press was told that the steel company was at work on "structural steel for bridges to replace those destroyed in Europe" and that shipment of the girders was being made by way of Canada.[9] Schwab's subterfuge was in full operation. But who was being fooled? To answer that question we turn back to Washington and the Department of State.

In the United States it is difficult for a government or a company to maintain absolute secrecy on an affair of more than

7. *Wall Street Journal* (December 24, 1914); see also the *Montreal Daily Star* (December 24, 1914).

8. Executive Committee Minutes, Canadian Vickers, Ltd., December 19, 28, 29, 1914, and January 11, 1915. Six keels were laid by January 14 and all ten were down by February 9.

9. *Wall Street Journal* (January 12, 1915).

trivial dimensions. This certainly was the case with the clandestine submarines. As we have seen, any regular reader of the
newspapers, especially the *Wall Street Journal,* in December
1914 could find evidence that the submarine episode was not
closed. When newspaper accounts of Schwab's rapid peregrina-
tions—Washington, Montreal, New York, London—were
coupled with the information received in the State Department
from Naval Intelligence sources about continued activity in
Bethlehem shipyards, suspicions were bound to arise. Only
three days after issuing his public statement about the cancelation Secretary Bryan conferred with Lansing about his suspicions,[10] and Lansing thereupon questioned James Hayden,
the Bethlehem lawyer. Hayden, a few days later, replied bland-
ly that there was no contract "for the construction of submarines, or the manufacture of materials suitable for use in the
construction of submarines, to be delivered by a citizen of the
United States to one of the belligerent powers." The statement
which Schwab made to Bryan, said Hayden, disposed of the
matter. Hayden's letter was written the day after Schwab signed
the supplementary contract at the Admiralty.[11]

Lansing did not challenge this statement, but he was under
no illusions. He knew the open secret that Bethlehem was indeed supplying "materials suitable for use in the construction
of submarines" for a belligerent. But what could be done about
it? As a lawyer Lansing was bothered by the gap between the
president's order and the government's lack of legal power to
enforce a genuine cancelation of the Bethlehem contract. Although nothing could be done legally at the moment, Lansing
concluded that the neutrality laws of the United States required
alteration to meet this special case. In a revealing memorandum
entitled "For Future Consideration: NEUTRALITY LAWS" Lansing outlined his thoughts:

> In addition to the present prohibition against outfitting
> or arming a ship or vessel for a belligerent government

10. Lansing desk diary, December 10, 1914, Lansing MSS.

11. Hayden to Lansing, December 16, 1914, Department of State file
763.72111 E1/1.

there should be a statute prohibiting under severe penalties the building, contracting to be built, or causing to be built a warship or other vessel for a belligerent, and the manufacturing of . . . any part of the hull, equipment or armament of a warship or any other vessel for a belligerent provided such warship, vessel, or parts are to be delivered in time of war.

At first glance the doctrine which Lansing thus advocated appears to contradict his earlier agreement with the principle that the rights of neutrals should be as extensive and their obligations as light and limited as possible. It is true that Lansing now was arguing that the United States should assume a new obligation to prevent the export of parts of vessels, but his argument was based not on abstractions, not on the vague spirit of law as in Wilson's case, but on the application of national self-interest to modern conditions of maritime warfare. "Self-interest," he wrote, ". . . is sufficient ground to prohibit any action which may increase a belligerent's power on the high seas. . . . As long as private property on the high seas is not immue from confiscation, and as long as commerce, even in non-contraband, is the prey of belligerents, a neutral should not aid a belligerent, even remotely, to increase its naval force."[12] This argument, of course, could easily be carried a step further. Would not a neutral supplying aid of any kind to a belligerent be helping that belligerent—even if remotely—to increase its naval force? If a belligerent could acquire its land armaments from neutrals, it could devote its own internal resources to naval expansion. Lansing, however, would not take this step, for he felt that a total embargo on armaments would place small peaceful nations at the mercy of well prepared aggressors by denying them access to arms.[13]

All this, however, was speculation. Lansing's thoughts are interesting as an example of the difficulty of applying the doctrine of self-interest to neutral behavior, but thoughts alone had

12. Memorandum of December 23, 1914, ibid., 763.72111/1430.
13. Memorandum of December 22, 1914, ibid.

no influence on the progress of Schwab's submarines. During January and February the Department of State was able to follow that progress without difficulty, thanks to reports sent on by the Navy Department. At Groton, Connecticut, British naval personnel were reported inspecting forty submarine engines being constructed for twenty submarines which the Admiralty had ordered.[14] From San Francisco came word that 90 per cent of the labor force of the Union Iron Works was employed on the building of "H" type submarines; that as of February 4 the work was half complete; that finished material was constantly being shipped to an unknown destination rumored to be Montreal; and that the general manager, the secretary, the assistant outside superintendent, the chief tool maker, and several ship fitters had left about the first of the year and also were rumored to be in Montreal.[15] An inquiry from the Department of State to the Deputy Commission of Corporations revealed the information, apparently previously not known, that the Union Iron Works was a subsidiary of the Bethlehem Steel Corporation.[16]

With information about Schwab's subterfuge so readily available, it was to be expected that the German and Austrian embassies would complain about what was taking place. Constantin Dumba, the Austrian ambassador, was the first to send an official protest. On January 26 he wrote Secretary Bryan:

> Now I hear from a reliable source that the Bethlehem plant sends secretly the component parts of submarines to Canada whence they are to be shipped to England. I consider this to be a flagrant violation of the duties of a neutral country and have the honour to protest against it expressing the

14. Inspector of Machinery, Groton, to Chief of the Office of Naval Intelligence, January 15, 1915, Department of State file 763.72111/1532.

15. Josephus Daniels to the Secretary of State, February 5, 1915, quoting report of the Supervisor, 12th Naval district, San Francisco, ibid., 763.72111/1609. The San Francisco *Examiner* and the *Chronicle* both carried extensive and surprisingly accurate accounts of developments at the Union Iron Works. See clippings preserved in files on "Foreign Submarines" in the Archives of the Electric Boat Division of the General Dynamics Corporation, Submarine Library, Groton, Connecticut.

16. Handwritten note on Daniels' letter, ibid.

conviction that Your Excellency will without loss of time, take all necessary steps to stop this underhand circumvention of . . . the President.[17]

The next day Count von Bernstorff, the German ambassador, supported his colleague and ally with a similar protest.[18]

These formal protests from the Central Powers added a new dimension to the affair. For the next several days the submarines were the major topic of concern within the Department, with Bryan, Lansing, and William Phillips, third assistant Secretary of State, holding one conference after another on the subject.[19] Bryan promised Bernstorff that his complaint was receiving "the most thorough investigation."[20] Thorough investigation, in this case, meant a letter from Bryan to Schwab asking directly if there was any truth to the German and Austrian accusations.[21] Schwab answered that he would be glad to come to Washington to talk to Bryan about the matter but that he was "unfortunately suffering from a bad cold" and could not leave New York. Schwab, however, did ask Paul D. Cravath, the Bethlehem Steel Corporation's general counsel, who was planning to be in Washington on other business, to see Bryan the following Saturday, February 6.[22]

Cravath, "a massive man of handsome presence, strong personality, and confidence in his own judgment,"[23] was one of the most prominent corporation lawyers of his day. Once a

17. Dumba to Bryan, January 26, 1915, ibid., 763.72111 E1 1/3. Apparently the Austro-Hungarian and German ambassadors had verbally indicated their intention of raising the submarine issue, for Colonel House discussed the matter with Wilson on January 24, 1915. See the entry for that date in House's diary, House Collection.

18. Bernstorff to Bryan, January 27, 1915, Department of State file 763.72111/1548.

19. Lansing Desk Diary, January 26, 27, February 1, 2, 1915.

20. Bryan to Bernstorff, February 3, 1915, Department of State, *Foreign Relations of the United States, 1915*, p. 781.

21. Bryan to Schwab, February 1, 1915, Department of State file 763.72111/2072.

22. Schwab to Bryan, February 4, 1915, ibid.

23. Article on Cravath in *Dictionary of American Biography,* Supplement II.

partner of Charles Evans Hughes and later, after the entry of
the United States into the war, to become a diplomatic representative in Europe of the Treasury Department, he was the
sort of man who could deal easily with a fellow lawyer like
Lansing but less successfully with a man like Bryan, whose
emotions were vague and who was known to be biased against
both big business and the munitions trade. Cravath called at
the Department on Saturday as promised. For the second time
in the recurring negotiations over the submarines Bethlehem
Steel's good fortune decreed that Bryan was absent from the
Department. As had been the case when James Hayden first
mentioned the submarines to the Department in November,
Lansing was again Acting Secretary of State. The two lawyers
conferred.[24]

Apparently no written record of the Cravath-Lansing conversation was made, but from the course of subsequent events
we can make reasonable inferences as to what was said. Cravath
must have admitted that Bethlehem Steel was building submarines in Canada with American materials; that fact, after
all, was common knowledge. But did materials constitute component parts? Lansing doubtless hoped to avoid a showdown
on the question of component parts when the government's
legal position was so weak. Cravath, in turn, must have hoped
to avoid a public collision between Bethlehem Steel and the
Federal government. In normal years the government was the
Bethlehem's best customer. Compromise and tacit understanding was in the interest of both parties. The specific point on
which an understanding was needed was the definition of what
constituted parts of submarines. When Cravath left Lansing's
office, such an understanding had been reached: if the materials
being shipped to Canada required further fabrication before a
submarine could be launched, then the State Department would
consider the materials as ordinary commercial products and
not as component parts of vessels of war. This understanding
was never put into writing and Secretary of State Bryan may

24. Lansing desk diary, February 6, 1915.

never have been aware of its existence, but Lansing was. In all subsequent discussions the understanding was followed as faithfully as if it had been written into law.

Probably following Cravath's advice, Schwab during the next week secured a letter from P. L. Miller, the general manager of Canadian Vickers, which stated Canadian Vickers was building submarines with materials purchased "wherever the orders can be placed most advantageously. We are making no purchases from the Bethlehem Steel Company itself, and our purchases from its subsidiary companies are comparatively insignificant."[25] Schwab then wrote Bryan and denied absolutely the truth of the charges by the Austrian and German ambassadors. As proof of his denial, Schwab enclosed the letter from Miller which, of course, was entirely misleading in its implication that Canadian Vickers was building submarines on its own responsibility and, while shopping for materials on the open market, just happened to make a few insignificant purchases from some Bethlehem Steel subsidiaries.

Schwab did state in his own letter that ten submarines were under construction by the Fore River Shipbuilding Company but that they would not be delivered to a belligerent nation during the war. "They are being built because before we received the President's request to abandon our contract we had invested a very large amount of money in materials which could only be used for component parts of submarines, and rather than sacrifice this investment" it was decided to complete the vessels but not deliver them. Schwab, of course, was referring to the second ten submarines in the original contract whose form and timing of delivery had been left indefinite with the Admiralty because of the "diplomatic situation."

There is no evidence that Bryan read this letter from Schwab or its enclosure from Miller, but Lansing did and gave instructions to the Department's diplomatic draftsman that a reply be prepared for the German ambassador on the basis of Schwab's letter, but with no reference whatsoever to the Canadian opera-

25. Miller to Schwab, February 10, 1915, enclosed in Schwab to Bryan, February 11, 1915, Department of State file 763.72111/1635.

tions. This reply went out on February 17, in the form of a letter from Bryan to Bernstorff. "I have ascertained that no component parts are being built by the Bethlehem Steel Works and being sent to Canada," the letter stated.[26]

In the narrowest technical sense the Department's reply to Bernstorff was not incorrect. According to Lansing's tacit definition the materials going to Canada from the Bethlehem works were not parts, since they required further manufacturing; furthermore, they were going not directly from "the Bethlehem Works" in Pennsylvania but from the shipbuilding subsidiaries. Assembled components such as engines were going not from any Bethlehem company but from subcontractors—the Electric Boat Company, for example. The Department was guilty not of lying but of dissimulation.

If we ask again who was fooled by Schwab's subterfuge, the answer is not the Department of State (although Bryan's incapacity for detailed work may have kept him uninformed), not the press (which carried surprisingly full reports), and not Great Britain's enemies. Ironically, only the Canadian government—whose interests were most directly involved—was at first totally unaware of the actual state of affairs. Thus the next and crucial stage of the story deals with the behavior of the Canadian government after they discovered what was happening.

26. Bryan to Bernstorff, February 17, 1915, ibid.

7 Canadian Anger

All arrangements for putting Schwab's subterfuge into operation were made among the Bethlehem Steel Corporation, the
Vickers companies in Great Britain and Canada, the British
government, and, tacitly, the American Department of State.
At no stage of the negotiation was the Canadian government
consulted or even informed, and this notwithstanding the fact
that there were at least four grounds on which Ottawa could
claim a direct interest in the affair. Since 1912, and more in-
tensively since the outbreak of war, as we have seen, the Canadian government had been importuning the Admiralty to place
contracts for warships directly in Canada; now they were being
ignored. Secondly, the submarines were causing work in progress for the Canadian government to be summarily discontinued.
Thirdly, the importation of American workers was a violation
of the Canadian Alien Labour Act. Finally, the situation threatened to entangle Canada, without the government's knowledge,
in difficulties with her neighbor, the United States.

For these reasons Prime Minister Sir Robert Borden was filled
with anger and disillusionment when he learned at long last
of the subterfuge. The knowledge of the many ways in which
the Canadian government had been flagrantly disregarded
rankled. Borden never forgot the circumstances of the Schwab
submarines and, as this chapter will show, he made the episode
a symbol of his drive for greater recognition by London of
Canada's national status and specific economic interests.

Borden, it will be recalled, had reacted with eager expectation to Secretary of State Bryan's much-publicized announcement that Schwab's submarine contract would not be fulfilled. While Schwab was explaining his proposed subterfuge to the Admiralty, Borden—unaware that Schwab had visited the Canadian Vickers plant—cabled to London urging that the submarines be built by a Canadian firm or firms in Canada. This communication was never acknowledged, for the Admiralty was too busy arranging matters according to Schwab's plan. On January 1 the Canadian Vickers plant came completely under the control of Bethlehem Steel, all work on the Canadian government's icebreaker stopped, and American workmen and materials began to come into Montreal. As of that date the Canadian government had received no communications on the subject from any source, and apparently neither Borden nor anyone else in a position of responsibility had read or attached any significance to the newspaper reports of Schawb's mysterious travelings.

One reason for Borden's overlooking the poorly concealed course of events may have been that he was concentrating his attention during the month of December 1914 on the large question of Canada's political status within the Empire and particularly the question of Dominion participation in fundamental decisions of foreign policy. This phase of Borden's leadership cannot be overlooked, for it was inextricably involved with his economic policies. The struggle to be heard politically and the struggle to be recognized economically were two sides of the same coin of Canadian national interest as defined by Borden.

By coincidence Borden happened to make one of the more forceful public expressions of his views in Montreal, December 7, 1914, at the very moment that Schwab was crossing the Atlantic to complete plans so demeaning to the Canadian government. Speaking to the students of McGill University, he said:

There is only one respect in which we in Canada have not yet attained our full share in self-government in this Em-

1. Parts crated by Electric
   Boat Company before
   shipment to Montreal.

2. Parts being unloaded at
   Canadian Vickers.

3. Submarine nearing com-
pletion at Canadian
Vickers.

4. Submarine after launching at Canadian Vickers.

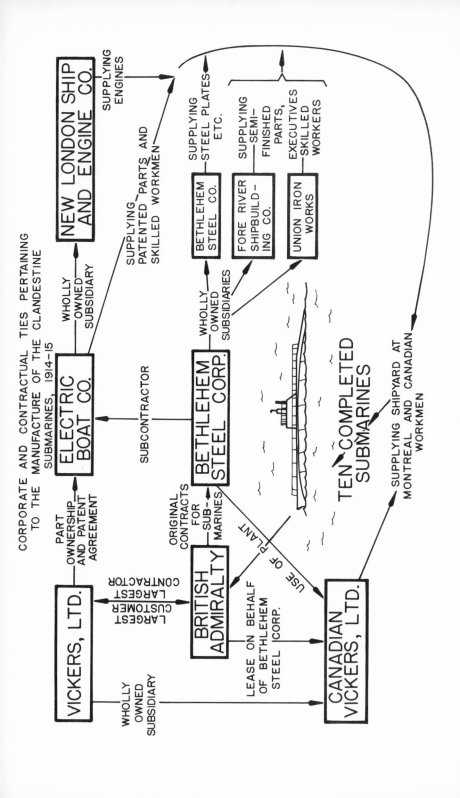

CORPORATE AND CONTRACTUAL TIES PERTAINING TO THE MANUFACTURE OF THE CLANDESTINE SUBMARINES, 1914–15

NEW LONDON SHIP AND ENGINE CO.

SUPPLYING ENGINES

SUPPLYING PATENTED PARTS AND SKILLED WORKMEN

SUPPLYING STEEL PLATES ETC.

SUPPLYING SEMI– FINISHED PARTS, EXECUTIVES SKILLED WORKERS

BETHLEHEM STEEL CO.

FORE RIVER SHIPBUILD– ING CO.

UNION IRON WORKS

WHOLLY OWNED SUBSIDIARY

ELECTRIC BOAT CO.

WHOLLY OWNED SUBSIDIARIES

SUBCONTRACTOR

BETHLEHEM STEEL CORP.

TEN COMPLETED SUBMARINES

SUPPLYING SHIPYARD AT MONTREAL AND CANADIAN WORKMEN

PART OWNERSHIP AND PATENT AGREEMENT

ORIGINAL CONTRACTS FOR SUB– MARINES

USE OF PLANT

VICKERS, LTD.

LARGEST CUSTOMER LARGEST CONTRACTOR

BRITISH ADMIRALTY

LEASE ON BEHALF OF BETHLEHEM STEEL CORP.

WHOLLY OWNED SUBSIDIARY

CANADIAN VICKERS, LTD.

pire, and that is with regard to foreign relations—the decision of those questions of alliances and understandings
which in the end must determine the issues of peace and
war. [The day must come] when the men of Canada, Australia, South Africa and the other dominions will have the
same just voice in these questions as those who live within
the British Isles. Any man who doubts that that will come,
doubts that the Empire will hold together.[1]

These thoughts Borden reiterated and elaborated upon in a
series of major speeches across Canada. His purpose was to in-
spire his audiences with the same vision of a politically mature
and self-reliant nation that was his own great goal. In the process he hoped to encourage the people to increase their efforts
in the present war, which, he thought, would hasten the completion of nationhood. But while the prime minister's thoughts
soared to such abstract and alluring realms, he was not unaware
of the development of a more mundane type of limitation on
Canada's self-government: the limitation represented and symbolized by the Schwab submarines. Before the war was over,
the accumulation of such affairs was to exert a greater influence
on Canada's relations with Great Britain than a thousand
speeches on the theoretical necessity of sharing in the making
"of alliances and understandings."

Not until January 6, 1915, was the first message on the affair
received by the government in Ottawa, but that message—a
telegram from Ambassador Spring-Rice in Washington to the
Governor-General—was vague and partially inaccurate. The
telegram said that fifteen of the original twenty submarines
would be completed in Montreal, that parts were en route to
Montreal by rail, and that the contractor, Bethlehem Steel, had
been warned to avoid all publicity regarding construction in
Canada. There was no word in the telegram of the Canadian
Vickers company, of the fact that American workers as well as
parts were going across the line, or of the necessity of setting

1. *Montreal Daily Star* (December 8, 1914).

aside work under contract from the Canadian government in order to make way for the submarines.[2]

Spring-Rice's telegram of January 6 appears to have been overlooked by Borden, for it was not until nine days later that he learned—from Canadian Vickers—about the submarines. Vickers told him that their works had been taken over by the British government, that American workmen were being brought in, and that the Company assumed that the Canadian government would receive notification in due course from the Colonial Office. Borden's first reaction on receiving this news was to think of the protests that might be expected from Canadian labor against illegal competition. Only the month before, Borden had incurred the displeasure of the Montreal Trades and Labour Council when he had replied negatively to the Council's plea for new public expenditure to provide jobs. All government funds, Borden had said, were going for war expenses; he deplored the terrible unemployment, but there was little, he said, that could be done from Ottawa.[3]

Legally the case against the importation of foreign workers was strong. Under the Canadian Alien Labour Act of 1906 it was unlawful to import a foreign worker under any contract or agreement, expressed or implied, made prior to the worker's immigration. A separate action could be instituted against a violator for each individual worker illegally brought into Canada, and the penalty for each violation was a fine of not more than $1,000 or less than $50. Upon conviction the person bringing the action against the violator might, under some circumstances, be awarded the sums forfeited as fines.[4] Thus, if the Montreal Trades and Labour Council sought to make an issue of the submarine affair, a most embarrassing situation might

2. Spring-Rice to the Governor-General, telegram, January 6, 1915, Borden MSS.

3. *Montreal Daily Star* (December 19, 1914).

4. *The Criminal Code of Canada, 1915*, pp. 1386–91. Although Borden appears to have had no doubts on the matter, the Bethlehem Steel Corporation might have been acquitted, if brought to trial, of violation of the Alien Labour Act. Section 9 (b) of the Act allowed the engaging of foreign workers under contract "to perform labour in or upon any new industry not at pres-

be created, a situation that would reflect ignominiously on his ability to maintain Canada's status and even prevent violation of Canada's laws.

Borden hastily cabled to High Commissioner Perley in London asking for confirmation of what he had learned from Vickers. A public announcement based on official information, Borden said, would mitigate "labour difficulties occasioned by bringing workmen from the United States."[5] Perley went immediately to the Admiralty, where he talked with Churchill's secretary and with the director of contracts. The Admiralty confirmed Borden's information but urged that no public announcement be made lest "international complications" arise over the importing of materials for the submarines from the United States.[6] Borden thus was put in a difficult position with no room to maneuver. He had to keep silent. If he told the full story, he could head off possible labor protests, but he might then endanger Schwab's subterfuge, and prevent the submarines from being built at all. Furthermore, a public disclosure would in all probability exacerbate the general tenor of Anglo-American relations, already seriously strained by American resentment against British efforts to restrict the trade of neutrals with Germany.

Meanwhile the Colonial Office, prodded by the Canadian High Commissioner, dispatched a long overdue official message. This cable, although vague, did give Borden more information. The colonial secretary said that "diplomatic considerations" required the abandonment of the original plan for constructing the submarines in the United States. Under the new scheme, however, Bethlehem Steel remained the responsible contractor. All this had been arranged in London between the Admiralty and Vickers representatives in London. The colonial

---

ent established in Canada" if workers could not be otherwise obtained. Certainly a good case could be made that the manufacture of submarines was a new industry under the meaning of the Act. For a successful defense under section 9 (b) of an accused violator see *R. v. Disney*, 14 Can.Cr.Cas., 152.

5. Borden to Perley, telegram, January 15, 1915, Borden MSS.
6. Perley to Borden, telegram, January 16, 1915, ibid.

secretary added, with stuffy understatement, that it was feared
that the use of the Canadian Vickers plant for the submarines
would "somewhat unfavourably affect" the building of the Canadian government's icebreaker and dredger, but "His Majesty's
Government hope, as Admiralty judge it vitally necessary to
use every means for earliest possible delivery of submarines,
that any inconvenience will be excused." The affair, he concluded, was one of utmost secrecy.[7]

Borden and Perley were ready enough to excuse the specific
inconvenience, but not the principle involved. Since August
1914 the Canadian government had encountered increasing
difficulty in maintaining adequate communication with the
many departments of the British government responsible for
the conduct of the war. The submarine affair was but one of a
series of irritating events, but it symbolized, better than anything else which had yet occurred, all that Borden and Perley
considered wrong in the wartime relations of Canada and Great
Britain: the failure to convey vital information, the disregard
of Canadian interests, the cavalier way in which a technically
illegal arrangement was set in motion without consulting Ottawa, the way in which an American corporation stood to gain
the profit while the Canadian government bore the inconvenience. Perhaps the extraordinary demands of the war required
that the submarines be built in this fashion. But why could not
the Canadian government have been allowed to concur in the
crucial decisions before they were made? This question—touching a vital matter of status—was at the heart of Borden's and
Perley's irritation.

One obstacle to an improved relationship which the submarine affair amply demonstrated was the existence of the Colonial Office as the only official avenue of communication between Ottawa and London. In peacetime the Colonial Office
machinery caused the Canadian government little difficulty, for
the cable to London seldom carried matters of urgent importance. But with the outbreak of war the old machinery—ac-
customed to carrying birthday greetings, condolences on the

7. Colonial Secretary to the Governor-General, telegram, January 16,
1915, ibid.

passing of aged statesmen, and occasionally a notification that
a treaty had been ratified—suddenly was required to carry
hundreds of urgent and highly complicated messages, many
requiring specialized technical knowledge, all demanding immediate action, all bearing on vital interests of Canada or other
part of the Empire. Officially, the Canadian prime minister
could not even communicate directly with the Colonial Office.
Officially, all messages were sent by the Governor-General to
the colonial secretary in letters or cables which began: "My
advisers inform me that" or, less stiffly: "Following from my
Prime Minister." In time of war, when hours are as important
as peacetime weeks, this added formality was often burdensome
in the extreme.

Ideally, the Colonial Office ought to have done more than
receive the innumerable messages originating abroad; it ought
to have been aware of every development in every department
at home which affected a dominion or colony. But the office
could not keep up with the work. Perhaps the inspiration of a
man like Lloyd George as colonial secretary might have
achieved the impossible, but Lewis Harcourt, the incumbent,
was amiable, unenergetic, and uninspiring. The submarine affair was a typical result of such conditions.

Theoretically, the Borden government had found a way
around the obstruction of the Colonial Office: regular Canadian
representation on the Committee of Imperial Defence. Perley,
who began his duties as High Commissioner in London in the
summer of 1914, was the Canadian representative. He attended
one unimportant meeting before the outbreak of war, but that
was all. Shortly before he was to learn of the submarine affair
—and the timing is significant—Borden raised the issue of the
Committee of Imperial Defence. Why had Perley not been invited to attend? Colonel Maurice Hankey, secretary of the Committee, answered that Perley had not been invited because the
Committee as such had not met since July:

> As a matter of fact, on the outbreak of war the Cabinet was
> in almost daily session for many weeks. Many points that
> in time of peace would have come before the Committee

of Imperial Defence were decided at once by the Cabinet, which inevitably superseded the functions of the Committee. . . . Gradually, however, as the war progressed the machinery of the Committee was again involved, and Sub-Committees have from time to time been appointed to deal with a considerable number of questions. . . . Mr. Harcourt particularly asked me to mention that, so little has the work of the Sub-Committees affected the Overseas Dominions and Colonies that he himself has only attended one meeting since the outbreak of the war.

Hankey added that Prime Minister Asquith was considering calling the full Committee of Imperial Defence again, in which case a Canadian representative would be invited.[8]

This was a classic bureaucratic run-around. The Canadian government had insisted on taking part in decisions of war and peace as a corollary to participation in the defense of the Empire. But now that war had come, and with it Canadian participation, the organ by which the Canadian government was to have been kept informed had ceased to exist. High Commissioner Perley, upon reading Hankey's explanation, could do no more than reply "that it would be advisable and give satisfaction in Canada" if he were appointed to one or two of the subcommittees.[9] The next day Perley received Borden's initial inquiry about the submarines, and for several days thereafter the two issues were simultaneously under discussion, each complementing the other, each increasing the Canadian conviction that basic reforms were necessary.

Initially, Perley, having experienced in person the frustrations of dealing with a British government which appeared oblivious of Canada, was more angry than Borden at the submarine affair. Perley reminded Borden how the Canadian government had repeatedly asked that Canadian firms be given direct contracts for building submarines, but had never received a reply from the Admiralty. Now, without warning, the

8. Hankey to Perley, January 15, 1915, ibid.
9. Perley to Borden, January 15, 1915, ibid.

Admiralty had placed Canada in a most awkward position "regarding labour problems and international relations to say nothing of stopping work on ice breaker and dredger." The High Commissioner urged that Borden send a strong letter of protest.[10]

In Ottawa Borden was, at this stage, less exercised over the submarines than Perley. The prime minister was a slow-tempered man in whom indignation built up gradually. While Perley sputtered in London, Borden drafted a mild rebuke to be sent through official channels, i.e. from the Governor-General to the colonial secretary. The Canadian government, he said, gladly offered full cooperation in expediting the construction of the submarines, and welcomed the fact that the work was being carried on in a Canadian shipyard. In the muffled jargon of such communications he added that the government "would, however, be grateful if a somewhat earlier intimation could be given to them as to the intention of His Majesty's Government in such matters as it seemed inappropriate that an arrangement made by His Majesty's Government which involved work undertaken by the Company for [the Canadian] Government should in the first instance be communicated . . . by the Company itself."[11]

The comparative mildness of Borden's remonstrance is partially explained by the fact that the potential labor difficulties which had caused him so much concern a few days earlier had not materialized. Although American workers were being imported by Bethlehem Steel, they were all highly skilled specialists and were comparatively few in number. Meanwhile the labor force of Canadian workers at Canadian Vickers had swelled far beyond the low level maintained before the submarines. Within two weeks of the laying of the first submarine keel the work force had already reached 800 men and was increasing rapidly. As Borden commented to one of the officers of Canadian Vickers, it was "very fortunate that the additional

10. Ibid., telegram, January 20, 1915, ibid.
11. Governor-General to the Colonial Secretary, telegram, January 21, 1915, and telegram of same date from Borden to Perley, ibid.

work thus provided is available at the present juncture."[12] This employment, Borden cabled to Perley, was of course important and appreciated; while protesting on principle to the British government he did not wish to appear "ungracious."[13]

Meanwhile, the officers of Canadian Vickers made no effort to conceal their dissatisfaction with what was taking place. Frederick Orr Lewis, the man who had labored for nearly a decade to bring about the establishment of a naval shipbuilding industry for Canada, was especially irritated. Lewis was then in England acting as liaison between Canadian Vickers and the parent company. He wrote Borden, January 21, that much of his time in recent weeks had been taken up with the details of the submarine arrangement. Bitterly he observed that the situation "does seem contradictory after all the proposals which have been made for the building of submarines. . . . It is sincerely to be regretted in this whole matter that we were not the original contractors, but if the ends of the Empire are served and the boats ready for service, this is the one and only consideration to be regarded at the present time." Lewis, however, was interested in more than the present. Ever the salesman and booster, he drew consolation from the fact that "one would naturally think that in the future, some cognizance of this plant should be taken, as Canada has once more stepped into the breach to relieve a very serious situation." Furthermore, since the war had demonstrated the undoubted importance of submarines as "ships of the future," perhaps the Canadian government might like to consider ordering eight or ten on its own account for coast protection.[14]

Now that Ottawa had been officially informed, Canadian Vickers was free to ask formally for an extension on the building of the icebreaker. "We had made good progress on her, and hoped to be able to deliver her within the time specified in the Contract, but owing to the desire of the Admiralty to obtain these submarines as quickly as possible, and to the cabled in-

12. Borden to Sir Montague Allan, January 25, 1915, ibid.
13. Borden to Perley, telegram, January 21, 1915, ibid.
14. Lewis to Borden, January 21, 1915, ibid.

structions we received, we had to stop work on her altogether."[15]
Ironically, word was received in Montreal at that moment that
the *Earl Grey*, the icebreaker whose sale to Russia in September 1914 had made the completion of the vessel at Canadian
Vickers a matter of urgency, was lying disabled in Archangel.[16]

Borden replied favorably to the request for an extension of
time on the icebreaker.[17] Shortly thereafter the British government, having warned that precautions should be taken against
sabotage at the Montreal plant,[18] gracefully sent a message of
thanks for Canada's cooperation and then added an apology
for the exceptional circumstances which had prevented Ottawa
from being properly informed. Every effort would be made to
ensure that a repetition of the affair did not occur.[19] For the
moment the entire episode appeared to have been amicably
settled. But Borden, although slow to anger, had a long memory. "We are glad to have the Submarines built in Montreal,"
he wrote Perley late in February, "but some of the permanent
officials of the Admiralty require shaking up and they will receive it if anything like this again transpires."[20]

Borden's long memory plus a succession of further incidents
in the following months combined to keep alive the Canadian
government's sense of grievance. For example, on February 22
the delay on the icebreaker, which threatened to cause inconvenience if not hardship for Canadian navigation in the spring,
was discussed in the House of Commons. J. D. Hazen, the Minister of Naval Service, was forced to fend off criticism by an
oblique reference to "reasons honourable gentlemen will understand" which had produced the delay.[21]

Another small incident began on February 23 when Borden,
still anxious to secure benefits for home industry and apparent-

15. Sir Montague Allan to Borden, January 21, 1915, ibid.
16. *Montreal Daily Star* (January 22, 1915).
17. Borden to Allan, January 25, 1915, Borden MSS.
18. Colonial Secretary to the Governor-General, telegram, February 4,
1815, ibid.
19. Telegram, February 8, 1915, ibid.
20. Borden to Perley, February 19, 1915, ibid.
21. Canada, *House of Commons Debates*, February 22, 1915.

ly deciding that the Admiralty would be in a more receptive mood than before, cabled to London that the Grand Trunk Railway Company was ready to build submarines at their new dock at Prince Rupert, British Columbia. He also passed on the Company's suggestion that the Russian government be approached as a possible customer.[22] This time, at least, the Admiralty heeded Borden's message, but their reply was negative. The Grand Trunk Pacific, they said, could not possibly build submarines in the time required without supervision and machinery from Britain, and such were not available.[23] From the point of view of naval efficiency, the Admiralty's position was eminently reasonable, but another rebuff did not improve Borden's temper. On February 24 a haughty complaint was received from the Admiralty against the Canadian attitude.[24] While Borden was convinced that Admiralty officials required "shaking up," these same officials were acting as if they were the aggrieved parties.

Then in March the labor protest which Borden had long feared took place. The Plumbers' and Steamfitters' Union complained to the Montreal Trades and Labour Council that aliens were working at Canadian Vickers on two twelve-hour shifts. The Union asked the Council to approach Vickers and ask for an eight-hour day and the employment of local men. The president of the Council conferred with P. L. Miller, the general manager of Vickers, and was told that only 150 out of a total force of 1,780 were aliens "and these were necessary owing to their expert knowledge in certain lines."[25]

22. Borden to Perley, telegram, February 23, 1915, Borden MSS.
23. Perley to Borden, telegram, March 4, 1915, ibid.
24. Colonial Secretary to the Governor-General, February 24, 1915, enclosing a letter, dated February 20, 1915, from the Secretary of the Admiralty to the Under Secretary of State for the Colonies.
25. *Montreal Daily Star* (March 19, 1915). See also the *Labour Gazette, 15* (April 1915), 1150. In 1934 Lawrence Y. Spear, vice president of the Electric Boat Company, testified before the Nye Committee on the transfer of American workers into Canada. Some Canadians were employed, Spear said, but "the vital men we took from the United States." United States Senate, *Hearings before the Special Senate Committee on the Investigation of the Munitions Industry*, 74th Congress, 2d Session (39 vols. Washington, 1934–1937), *1*, 265–66.

The Trades and Labour Council remained dissatisfied, but they did not press their complaints. The work at Vickers proceeded rapidly, with the force working around the clock on long shifts. By early April the bulk of the work was nearing completion and the Canadian Vickers company was stressing the urgent need for additional work. Borden decided the time had arrived to ensure that the huge labor force which had accumulated would be kept employed after the submarines had departed. He told Perley to communicate with Churchill and make the strongest possible representations along the following lines:

> Submarines . . . will be completed very soon. This will throw over two thousand men out of employment. It is most desirable under present conditions that this should be avoided if possible. Vickers are prepared to construct at Montreal submarines, destroyers, or cruisers and will guarantee satisfactory delivery. Please urge upon Admiralty great importance giving Canadian Vickers reasonable share for any war craft of these classes required in immediate future . . . without delay as five or six hundred of the men now employed must otherwise be discharged within next two weeks. The action of British Government in requisitioning many Canadian ships has greatly lessened opportunities for employment in Montreal Harbour and therefore there is the greatest necessity to keep Vickers Works occupied.[26]

The allusion to the requisitioning of ships linked the submarine affair with another Canadian grievance against the British Government: the wholesale commandeering, without consulting Ottawa, of merchant ships in Canadian service. This practice, so disruptive of Canadian trade, was justified by the demands of the war. But to Ottawa it appeared that the Ad-

26. Borden to Perley, telegram, April 8, 1915; Perley immediately sent Churchill a copy of Borden's telegram, Perley to Churchill, April 9, 1915, Borden MSS. The first of the ten submarines was launched April 18 and the last May 26. Trials were completed between May 18 and June 20 and final delivery made on June 27. See Electric Boat Division of the General Dynamics Corporation Archives, Submarine Library, Groton, Connecticut.

miralty, as in the subterfuge concerning the submarines, was acting in a high-handed manner which ignored Canadian status and interests. Such were the mundane problems that lay beneath Canada's ever more insistent demands for recognition of her nationhood.

In London, Perley carried out his instructions. He conferred with Sir Frederick Black, the Admiralty director of contracts, who admitted that the building of the submarines was being carried out satisfactorily in Montreal. Thus encouraged, Perley wrote to Churchill: "Our farmers are in good shape, but the war has brought quite a lot of distress in the cities owing to the dislocation of ordinary business, and we are most anxious to keep unemployment at as low a figure as possible." Noting the urgent need for cargo shipping and the fact that British yards were working overtime, Perley urged placing contracts for merchant as well as war ships in Canada. "Now that a good staff has been got together in Montreal would it not be a great pity to have them disbanded.... I would ask your friendly consideration of the Prime Minister's request, which means so much to the city of Montreal and vicinity."[27]

Perley's argument was ably presented. In the light of the nearly disastrous shortage of shipping that developed in 1917 at the peak of the German submarine offensive, his suggestions for the building of merchant ships were of vital importance to Great Britain and the Empire. But Churchill, as so often in the past, gave an unfavorable reply. He ignored the question of merchant ships altogether and merely referred Perley to a letter written earlier to the Governor-General in which Churchill promised to arrange to have a Royal Navy cruiser repaired at Canadian Vickers.

Perley then prevailed upon Harcourt to present the Canadian case to Churchill, but the colonial secretary was equally unsuccessful. "I mentioned the Canadian Vickers matter to Mr. Churchill," Harcourt reported, "but he cannot do anything more about submarines. We have got apparently already com-

27. Ibid.

pleted or on order as many as we can use or the Seas will hold!
He also tells me that none of the parts of the submarines are
made in Canada but are sent in from the United States and
merely assembled in the Vickers Yard."[28]

Churchill's comments are of interest on two counts: first for
the reflection of changes in Admiralty thinking on the submarine and second for the light they throw on the delicate
question whether Schwab was or was not exporting component
parts in violation of his promise to the American government.
On the first point, Lord Fisher's prophecies had been fulfilled
by the spring of 1915, but with one serious qualification. The
submarine was the battleship of the future, but it was of no use
if your enemy was unable or unwilling to send vessels out on
the surface of the sea. The submarine was of slight value against
other submarines or fast-moving and alert warships. Against
merchant vessels it was devastating—a fact which was about
to be tragically emphasized by the German sinking of the *Lusitania*. But if one's enemy employed no merchant vessels outside
of protected waters, what need was there for an enormous number of submarines? Thus by April of 1915 Lord Fisher's crusade
for more submarines had lost its impetus. The Admiralty was
more than content with the ten vessels soon to be received from
Montreal and the others that would eventually be delivered by
builders in Great Britain. Even the second ten of the original
Schwab order were no longer needed; the Admiralty had decided to make no effort to take possession of them. Parenthet-
ically, it is interesting to note that Fisher himself never wavered
from his unqualified faith. In May 1915 he resigned from the
Admiralty and helped precipitate a political crisis which shook
the Asquith government and led to Churchill's removal as First
Lord. The new First Lord was Arthur Balfour, who shortly
appointed Fisher as head of a Special Inventions Board. Fisher
began to dream of a gigantic submarine carrying a sixteen-inch
gun which could be fired while the vessel was submerged. Balfour expressed interest but added, significantly, "at this mo-

28. J. Masterton Smith (Churchill's secretary) to Perley, April 12, 1915,
and Lewis Harcourt to Perley, April 14, 1915, ibid.

ment I would give up all the new submarines in the world if
the Inventions Board could discover a method of destroying the
old ones!!!"[29]

Churchill's comment that Canada's only contribution to the
submarines was to provide a site for the assembly of parts manufactured in the United States was both an insult to Canadian
skills and a partial untruth, because, as contemporary photographs of the construction of the submarines prove, the workmen in Montreal did far more than assemble fully finished
component parts. Churchill's remark does, however, illustrate
the impossibility of defining precisely the meaning of the word
"parts." Ironically, Churchill and German Ambassador Bernstorff were for different reasons in agreement that Schwab was
exporting completed parts—Bernstorff because he hoped for
intervention by the American government against the work in
Montreal or, failing that, for Anglo-American friction over the
affair; Churchill because he wanted to justify his refusal to give
Canadian yards full responsibility for carrying out a shipbuilding contract.

The negative result of Borden's efforts to get new contracts
for Canadian Vickers revived and exacerbated his irritation at
the original arrangement. Bitterly he wrote to Perley:

> We can of course say nothing in view of the Admiralty's
> decision that no further construction is required. Please
> note, however, that up to the present time neither Mr. Har-
> court nor Mr. Churchill has given any satisfactory, definite
> or reasonable answer as to why an order for these sub-
> marines was given to the United States when the British
> Government and especially the Admiralty knew perfectly
> well, and had been specially notified, that the submarines
> could be efficiently and promptly constructed in Canada.[30]

Notwithstanding Borden's bitter words, the Admiralty had explained why the order went first to the United States—namely

29. Balfour to Fisher, September 6, 1915, Fisher MSS.
30. Borden to Perley, April 26, 1915, Borden MSS.

that it seemed reasonable that the submarines could be built far more rapidly by an American company which had constructed submarines before and already had acceptable plans on hand.[31] That Borden did not consider this explanation satisfactory, definite, or reasonable is a measure of the degree to which the submarine affair, so prolonged and so continually irritating, had both stimulated his national pride and warped his judgment. Unconsciously, he was putting the specific interests of Canada before the broader interests of the Empire as a whole. Borden in April was far more a nationalist than he had been in January. The continued blindness of the Admiralty to the Canadian point of view was not the least of the factors driving him to this new position.

Late in April the first of the submarines was launched, less than four months after the keel had been laid and nearly four months ahead of schedule. Although the Canadian government, for the moment, suspended its efforts to induce the Admiralty to place further orders with Canadian Vickers, the submarines continued to produce friction between Ottawa and London— first, in regard to a potential crisis with the United States and, second, over a matter of naval defense for the city of Halifax. A discussion of these two aspects of the affair concludes the present chapter.

As the submarines neared completion in Montreal, Ambassador Spring-Rice in Washington became increasingly alarmed by German efforts to stimulate opposition in the United States to the export of munitions to the Allies. German propaganda, he said, was placing special emphasis on the submarines. He reported that a delegation had visited the State Department in order to protest against the export of finished parts to Canada, that spies were diligently taking photographs of the parts, and that a widespread outburst in the press was momentarily expected. "For us it is essential that we should be able to prove that parts of submarines made in the United States are not

31. Perley to Borden, telegram, April 9, 1915, ibid.

sufficient in themselves to make a complete submarine."[32] In response to the ambassador's warning the Colonial Office cabled Ottawa asking the Canadian government to furnish "all necessary information as soon as possible so that replies may be issued to any statement made by the German Embassy."[33] This request, placing on the Canadian government the responsibility for justifying an operation which had been concocted by Schwab and the Admiralty behind the Canadian government's back, was typical of wartime confusion in London. In this instance the Colonial Office did not know, or had forgotten, the role of the Admiralty in the affair.

Officially the Canadian government replied by reminding the Colonial Office "that all arrangements . . . were made by Admiralty who it is presumed will take action if necessary."[34] Unofficially, however, J. D. Hazen, the Minister of the Naval Service, ordered a thorough investigation. If difficulty should develop with the United States because of German charges, it might be advisable for the Canadian government to have its own information. Accordingly, G. J. Desbarats, the Deputy Minister of the Naval Service, visited the Vickers yard in Montreal, interviewed the officers of the company, and then traveled to New York, where he conferred with Sir Trevor Dawson of Vickers, Ltd., who happened at that time to be in the United States. Desbarats' long report, submitted May 3, 1915, is an important document in the history of the submarines, for it describes in detail the techniques of construction used for the vessels. Virtually all the materials for the submarines, Desbarats reported, were imported from the United States, but:

> It seems clear that the plates and shapes needed for the construction of the hulls were imported from the United States as absolutely raw material. No preparation was made

32. Spring-Rice to Governor-General, telegram, April 11, 1915 (addressed to Foreign Office, repeated to Canada), Borden MSS.

33. Colonial Secretary to the Governor-General, telegram, April 30, 1915, ibid.

34. Governor-General to the Colonial Secretary, telegram, May 4, 1915, ibid.

in the way of bending or shaping. . . . All the work of the construction of the hulls proper was done in the Vickers Yard at Montreal, and it, therefore, seems clear that it cannot be charged that any of these ships were practically built in the States and merely assembled in Canada.[35]

Ottawa was thus armed with information, but the German-inspired crisis which Spring-Rice feared never came. Four days after the submission of the Desbarats report the liner *Lusitania* was sunk by a German submarine. In Washington all lesser issues of foreign policy were submerged in the ensuing debate between the United States and Germany. By the time the sharp edge of the dispute was dulled weeks later, Secretary of State Bryan had resigned and Robert Lansing was in his place. With the elevation of Lansing, one of the principal architects of the submarine subterfuge, all chance of an effective German agitation against the submarines came to an end. The brief alarm, so ineptly handled in London, served only to diminish further Canadian faith in the ability of the British government to act competently where Canadian interests were concerned.

Another exchange between the Canadian and British governments in May 1915 constitutes perhaps the most absurd episode in the entire submarine affair. It happened that the director of the Canadian Naval Service, Vice-Admiral Charles E. Kingsmill, considered that the floating defenses of Halifax were insufficient. He had been trying unsuccessfully since November 1914 to convince the Admiralty to station at least two submarines there. The presence of the nearly completed submarines in Montreal, coming on top of Churchill's comment that the Admiralty had as many submarines as it could use or the seas would hold, suggested to Kingsmill that his efforts might now succeed. Could not two of the ten Vickers boats be assigned to Halifax? The Canadian government formally asked the Admiralty if this could be done, and further promised to build on

35. "Report on the construction of submarines at the works of Canadian Vickers Limited in connection with questions of the breach of neutrality, May 3, 1915," Borden MSS.

its own account two submarines at Canadian Vickers which, in a few months, could replace the pair stationed at Halifax.[36] Significantly this was the first time during the war that the Canadian government had offered to spend its own money on contracts with Canadian Vickers.

The Admiralty rejected the Canadian request and argued— quite sensibly from a naval point of view—that stronger defenses at Halifax were unnecessary. Canada was told to build her own submarines for Halifax, or—alternatively—Canada could have two of the ten submarines which Schwab was building in the United States, although "delivery of these may not be secured until after the war." If the Canadian government was willing to wait that long, the Admiralty offered to "transfer them at cost price."[37] How ludicrous to offer submarines after the war to meet what Canada considered an immediate danger from Germany! How disingenuous to offer at "cost price" vessels for which the Admiralty was committed to paying approximately twice the normal price! The Canadian government ignored the Admiralty's offer, and on that low note one phase of the history of the submarines came to an end.

During the summer of 1915 all ten of the submarines sailed overseas under their own power. Charles Schwab's contract for the Montreal boats was fulfilled. But the affair was not over. The dissatisfaction of the Canadian government persisted. As the following chapter will describe, that dissatisfaction at length brought important reforms.

36. Governor-General to the Colonial Secretary, telegram, May 3, 1915, ibid.

37. Colonial Secretary to the Governor-General, telegram, May 14, 1915, ibid.

8 Imperial Reforms

The episode of the clandestine submarines is a particularly vivid instance of the type of problem that daily confronted the Canadian government during the war. There were dozens of similar episodes, involving, for example, the sale of Canadian horses, the rejection by the British of Canadian-made rifles, the export of Canadian apples, and—most time-consuming and bothersome of all—the provision of adequate merchant shipping to meet Canadian needs. Another cluster of grievances revolved around the issue of whether Canadian or British officers would lead Canadian troops.

Together these problems raised basic questions concerning the relationship of Canada and Great Britain. What did it mean to be more than colony but less than equal partner in the midst of a great war? How could Canadian interests be advanced when the British government had sole responsibility for the over-all manner in which the Empire waged war? Should compromises be devised when special Canadian interests seemed to clash with British action, or should Canada always give way? By the spring of 1915 politicians in Ottawa and London were beginning to understand these questions, but they had not yet found any answers; indeed, Anglo-Canadian relations were destined to grow worse before the first reforms were successfully carried through. The path to reform can be traced by placing the history of the submarines in the larger context of wartime developments.

The truism that economic and political affairs cannot be separated applies in full measure to Anglo-Canadian difficulties during the war. At the same time that Prime Minister Sir Robert Borden and his colleagues sought greater recognition of Canada's economic position in the Empire, they desired also a voice in the larger political conduct of the war and of Imperial foreign policy in general. In both the economic and the political spheres Borden's goal was to advance Canada's national status by increasing her role in the affairs of the Empire. During the early part of the war he met little but frustration in both spheres.

The Canadian government in the summer of 1914 had no more information on the conduct of British foreign policy than was available in the newspapers. There had never been any effective consultation between London and the Dominions. When war broke out, Canada, along with her sister Dominions, went to war automatically. Although Borden accepted this situation as inevitable, he was determined that such circumstances should not arise again. Month after month in public speech and official and private correspondence, he reiterated his contention that henceforth the government of Canada must participate in the great questions of "alliances and understandings" which determine peace or war. The British response consisted of a vague promise—afterward quoted many times—from the Colonial Secretary to the Governor-General that "it is the intention of His Majesty's Government to consult . . . most fully, and if possible personally, when the time to discuss possible terms of peace arrives."[1] This promise for an indefinite future completely overlooked the fact that nothing so influences terms of peace as the conduct of war. Because no concrete reforms accompanied this promise, Borden's irritation at the lack of facilities for political consultation mounted through the winter and spring of 1915 in step with his growing dissatisfaction with Britain's inadequate recognition of Canada's economic interests. Communication and mutual understanding between the two

1. Telegram of January 21, 1915 quoted by Borden, Canada, *House of Commons Debates,* January 31, 1917.

governments was so poor that Borden at length concluded that only a personal visit to England might produce results.

Borden had excessive expectations as he set sail from New York at the end of June 1915. "I expect to hold several important conferences with the heads of the war departments over the placing or orders . . . in America," he told reporters as he boarded the *Adriatic*. "These orders have nearly all been placed in the United States, and Canada seems to have been neglected."[2] These conferences would surely lead to reform. Borden also seems to have been laboring under illusions in the political sphere. He expected the British government to know exactly what war conditions were, how long victory would take to achieve, and precisely how it would be gained. He seems to have felt that somewhere there was a secret master plan which would be unfolded before him. He would then become a full partner in the direction of the war; perhaps from his own experience he could offer some valuable advice. Then, armed with his new knowledge, he could return to Canada and lead the nation to victory in the war and permanently greater status in the world. It does not seem to have occurred to him that there might be no plan at all, or that the British government might be just as confused about the direction of the war as he was. The height of his illusions explains the depth of the bitterness that ultimately resulted from his mission.

Borden's visit began auspiciously, even romantically. Shortly after his arrival in London he was invited to attend a meeting of the Cabinet. Seated next to Prime Minister Herbert Asquith at the long polished table at 10 Downing Street, he listened to some pompous remarks about the great precedent that was being established: for the first time in history a colonial statesman was admitted to the sanctum of the Cabinet, to the very heart of the Empire.[3] Asquith then leaned toward Borden and reminded him of the sacred tradition that forbade the taking

2. *Wall Street Journal* (July 1, 1915).

3. *Times* (London) (July 15, 1915) hailed Borden's attendance at the Cabinet as a memorable landmark in the history of the Empire.

of any notes at Cabinet meetings. The atmosphere was impressive.[4]

The session of July 14 was the only Cabinet meeting that Borden attended. Rapidly the illusion of being a participant in the supreme direction of the war disappeared. Trivialities, not high policy, occupied most of his time.[5]

The effort to establish a new economic relationship, especially in regard to war orders, between Britain and Canada had equally disappointing results. Borden's discussion of the submarine issue typifies his experience. On the 12th of August he called at the Admiralty, determined to explain his grievances in the matter of the submarines in such a manner that repetition would be impossible. He conferred with Sir Graham Greene, secretary of the Admiralty.[6] Greene, who was not familiar with the details of the episode, seemed to question the accuracy of Borden's complaints, but he did promise to investigate. A week later, after investigation had confirmed what Borden said, Greene wrote what amounted to an apology: "The fact that the Vickers' officials at Montreal were admitted to a knowledge of this affair before your Government was consulted or apprised must have caused vexation and difficulties, and the Admiralty much regret that such an omission should have been made. I can only add that steps have been taken which will, it is hoped, make a similar unfortunate occurrence impossible."[7] Borden, having fastened tenaciously to what he considered a serious affront to Canada's status and interests, was not to be mollified. In reply to Greene he had the last word:

> I still fail to comprehend why our repeated communications with regard to Canadian facilities for building Submarines were utterly ignored or why no inquiry by the Admiralty was made in Canada before placing the order in the United States. Still less do I understand why the

4. Henry Borden, *Borden Memoirs, 1,* 500.
5. Ibid., pp. 497–509.
6. Borden diary, August 12, 1915, in possession of Henry Borden, Esquire, Toronto, Ontario.
7. Greene to Borden, August 20, 1915, Borden MSS.

Admiralty should have undertaken without consultations with us to postpone a contract made by Canadian Vickers, Ltd., with the Government of Canada. . . . the action of the Admiralty was a matter of public notoriety before we had the honour of being told that our contract was set aside without our consent. . . .

Indeed the explanation afforded in your letter is of so nebulous a character that I would hesitate to place it before the Canadian Parliament or people.[8]

At the end of August 1915 Borden prepared to return to Canada. Reviewing his trip, he reached a dismal conclusion: after weeks of discussion, of going "from pillar to post, from one member of the British Government to another," he possessed no more definite information than when he left Ottawa. Borden confronted Andrew Bonar Law, the Colonial Secretary (as of May 1915), and delivered what was virtually an ultimatum. Dramatically—if we can trust Borden's memory after the event—he told Bonar Law of his sense of frustration and threatened: "Unless I obtain this information which is due to me as Prime Minister of Canada, I shall not advise my countrymen to put further effort into winning the War. In three days time I am leaving and I now come to you for the purpose of conveying through you to the British Government the decision I have just announced." Bonar Law was alarmed, and said that there was only one man who could tell Borden what he wanted to know: Lloyd George, at that time head of the recently established Ministry of Munitions. Significantly, there was no mention of Prime Minister Asquith. Lloyd George was then resting in the country for a few days because of overexertion, but at Bonar Law's urging he came up to London and spent two hours with Borden going frankly and fully into Great Britain's position in the war, admitting many failures, and predicting that it would not be until the autumn of 1916 that the fully organized strength of the Empire would be applied to the war. This conversation with the man who had a better grasp of the

8. Borden to Greene, August 24, 1915, ibid.

requirements of the war than any other member of the Cabinet served two purposes: it mollified Borden for the moment, causing him to withdraw his threat about not urging Canada to continue its efforts in the war; and it laid the foundation for the close cooperation which developed between Borden and Lloyd George after the latter became the British Prime Minister in December 1916.[9]

Back in Ottawa, however, Borden found that relations with the British government were unchanged. There were promises and platitudes, but no new flow of information, no reforms in the machinery of Imperial relations. The climax of Borden's discontent in the political sphere came in January 1916. A letter which he wrote to High Commissioner Perley so well expresses his feelings that it deserves quotation at length:

> During the past four months since my return from Great Britain, the Canadian Government (except for an occasional telegram from you or Sir Max Aitken) have had just what information could be gleaned from the daily Press and no more. As to consultation, plans of campaign have been made and unmade, measures adopted and apparently abandoned and generally speaking steps of the most important and even vital character have been taken, postponed or rejected without the slightest consultation with the authorities of this Dominion.
>
> It can hardly be expected that we shall put 400,000 or 500,000 men in the field and willingly accept the position of having no more voice and receiving no more consideration than if we were toy automata. Any person cherishing such an expectation harbours an unfortunate and even

9. Borden subsequently prepared two accounts of these all-important interviews with Bonar Law and Lloyd George; one for the *Memoirs, 1,* 507–08, and the other in a letter to Lord Beaverbrook, July 5, 1928, Borden MSS. In both accounts Borden quotes directly and at length from his remarks to Bonar Law; the quotations agree in substance but not in exact phraseology. Both accounts agree in tone and content with direct, contemporary evidence of what Borden was saying and thinking at the time. Borden's diary, August 21 and 24, 1915, confirms that the discussions took place.

dangerous delusion. Is this war being waged by the United Kingdom alone, or is it a war waged by the whole Empire? If I am correct in supposing that the second hypothesis must be accepted then why do the statesmen of the British Isles arrogate to themselves solely the methods by which it shall be carried on in the various spheres of warlike activity and the steps which shall be taken to assure victory and a lasting peace?

It is for them to suggest the method and not for us. If there is no available method and if we are expected to continue in the role of automata the whole situation must be reconsidered.[10]

This letter marks the worst moment for Anglo-Canadian relations of the war. By writing it, Borden seems to have released pent-up tensions, and almost immediately thereafter the situation began to improve; indeed, even as Borden wrote, important reforms in wartime economic relations were being instituted.

Scarcely had Borden returned to Ottawa in September 1915 than he discovered an affair that in some ways was a carbon copy of the submarine episode: the Admiralty had placed an order for 500 patrol boats with the Electric Boat Company in the United States without giving Canadian firms a chance to bid. As with the submarines, the Electric Boat Company shipped parts and machinery to Canada, where the boats were assembled in local yards. Borden, as was to be expected after the assurances received from the Admiralty in August, exploded with a barrage of telegrams almost as numerous and acrimonious as those sent in regard to the submarines. The Admiralty's explanation was that the order for patrol boats had been placed in July 1915, before the correspondence between Borden and Sir Graham Greene.[11] The episode was the last of its kind during the war.

The reason that there was not an endless series of submarine

10. Borden to Perley, January 4, 1916, *Memoirs, 1,* 622.
11. Arthur Balfour to Bonar Law, November 6, 1915, copy in Borden MSS.

and patrol boat affairs is that the establishment in Canada of the Imperial Munitions Board made possible a major reform in economic relations. The story can be briefly told. Through the first year of the war one of the obstacles to the placing of orders in Canada was the lack of an adequate organization for the supervision and control of production. In England the War Office was too hampered by traditional ways to meet the requirements of munitions supply under revolutionary conditions of twentieth-century warfare. The Admiralty, as we have seen, also had its inadequacies. In May 1915 a scandalous shortage of artillery shells was revealed to the British public; as a result the responsibility for munitions was transferred from the War Office to the specially created Ministry of Munitions under Lloyd George.[12] In Canada, however, munitions production continued for six unsatisfactory months, dominated personally by the flamboyant and unstable Sir Sam Hughes, Minister of Militia and Defence, and a group of aides known as the "Shell Committee."

The Committee's work, substantial as it was in some respects, was subject to heavy and justifiable criticism. Orders were distributed in an arbitrary manner, costs were high and irregular, production schedules uncertain, inspection defective. Hughes, unable to tell a patriot from a profiteer, surrounded himself with men of notorious reputation. Worst of all, the British Ministry of Munitions found working with Hughes and the Committee an impossible task. The Committee, oriented almost exclusively to the manufacture of munitions in the narrowest sense, ignored the vital question of shipbuilding.[13]

The sequence of events that led to the replacement of the Shell Committee began in the summer of 1915 at the time of Borden's trip to England, when Lloyd George sent D. A. Thomas

12. For Lloyd George's own slashing but documented account of the failings of the War Office and the establishment of the Ministry of Munitions see his *War Memoirs* (6 vols. Boston, 1933–37), *1*, 112–308.

13. David Carnegie, *The History of Munitions Supply in Canada, 1914–1918* (Toronto, 1925), is useful but does not deal adequately with the controversial nature of the Shell Committee.

(afterward Lord Rhondda), Welsh coal magnate, to the United States and Canada in order to organize North American munitions production. Borden, on returning from England, found Thomas slow and difficult to deal with.[14] Thomas was critical of the Shell Committee, but failed to propose any acceptable changes. His one suggestion, that an Englishman be brought to Canada to act as chairman, was opposed by Borden.[15] In October 1915 (incidentally at the height of the patrol boat controversy) Thomas went back to England, having accomplished nothing.[16]

At this point the British Ministry of Munitions turned the problem over to two disciples of Lord Milner and members of the influential Round Table movement for greater Imperial unity: R. H. Brand and Lionel Hichens. The selection was singularly appropriate. Both were young, forceful, and efficient. Dedicated to the ideal of Imperial unity, they were sensitive to the national aspirations of the Dominions and aware of the affronts which those aspirations had recently suffered. Both realized that Canada was in danger of moving toward separation unless her legitimate interests were satisfied within the Empire. Acting on this assumption, the two men were determined that there would be no further unwarranted neglect of Canadian industry.

Brand and Hichens departed immediately for Canada, where they made a favorable impression on Borden. After deciding that the Shell Committee had to go, they presented Borden with an alternative: either a ministry of munitions in the Canadian government or an agency of the British Ministry in Canada. Borden chose the second.[17] Perhaps he felt that a British agency, staffed with Canadians, would represent a clear break from the

14. Borden diary, September 22, 1915.
15. Ibid.
16. The background to the Thomas mission is described in a long and informative memorandum, dated March 6, 1917, on the Imperial Munitions Board prepared by R. H. Brand, in the J. W. Flavelle MSS, Public Archives of Canada, Ottawa.
17. Ibid.

Shell Committee and be more effective in communicating with London. If these were his thoughts, they proved correct.

Arrangements for the formation of the new agency, styled the Imperial Munitions Board, were completed by November 24, 1915. Joseph W. Flavelle, industrialist, financier, and cogent critic of the Shell Committee, consented to be the Board's chairman, with full authority over the production of munitions in Canada.[18] The Board easily established harmonious relations with the Canadian government, which is not difficult to explain, since six of the seven Board members were Canadians; the seventh was Colonel David Carnegie, formerly technical adviser to the Shell Committee. Brand was the Board's representative at the Ministry of Munitions in London. His skilled and persistent advocacy quickly brought recognition of the principle that no munitions orders would be placed in the United States if they could be filled in Canada.[19] Month by month the volume of Canadian production mounted, costs went down, the bitter complaints of neglect in favor of the United States disappeared. Gradually Canadian factories turned to the production of ever heavier and more complex munitions. The Shell Committee had dealt mainly in shell casings; the Imperial Munitions Board encouraged the manufacture of the complete projectile, many as large as nine inches in diameter. By the end of 1916 the Board had established an airplane factory which ultimately produced 2,900 machines. Also late in 1916 the Board, as agent for the new British Ministry of Shipping, began to place orders for steel and wooden cargo ships in Canada, at last giving some substance to Borden's dream of stimulating Canadian shipbuilding. When the United States entered the war, the Board established an office in Washington and, before the Armistice, delivered $32 million worth of munitions to the United States, in pleasing contrast to the earlier jealousy over American production. An additional $145 million

18. For Flavelle's criticism of the Shell Committee see his correspondence with Borden during the spring of 1915, Flavelle MSS.
19. Memorandum by Brand, February 28, 1917, ibid.

worth of American orders were canceled because of the Armistice.[20]

The remarkably improved economic relationship brought about by the work of the Imperial Munitions Board prepared the way for changes in the political sphere. Again Lloyd George must receive the principal credit for reforms on the British side. As Minister of Munitions in 1915 he called on men like Hichens, Brand, and Flavelle, who made the Imperial Munitions Board succeed. As Prime Minister from December 1916 onward, he drew on the ideas of many men to create the institutions which finally brought the Dominions, and Canada in particular, into that close political relationship of consultation and cooperation which Borden had sought so long in vain in the early years of the war. The history of the Imperial War Conferences and the Imperial War Cabinet is beyond the scope of this study, but they are significant as institutions which developed from the political and economic discontent, from that sense of neglect and injured national pride, which the episode of the clandestine submarines symbolized.

20. The details of Board operations can be followed in the voluminous Flavelle papers. The best summary of the Board's work is Flavelle's final report, dated August 21, 1921, to the Minister of Munitions, copy in Flavelle MSS.

9 *Further American Repercussions*

In the previous chapter we saw how the submarine affair lay at the center of a complex tangle of economic and political problems in the Anglo-Canadian relationship, and how the important reforms devised during the war in that relationship were designed to prevent the type of fiasco which the submarines so vividly symbolized. The present chapter returns to the policy of the American government and to the echoes of the affair which continued to reverberate in the United States long after the original ten submarines in Canada had been completed.

The Department of State, it will be recalled, in February 1915 absolutely denied the charge of German Ambassador Bernstorff that Bethlehem Steel was exporting components of submarines for assembly in Canada. This denial was grounded on dissimulation and on some hair-splitting definitions, but not on absolute falsehood. Additional illumination is thrown on the Department's policy by its handling of a complaint received from the Lake Torpedo Boat Company of Bridgeport, Connecticut.

This company was the principal competitor of Bethlehem Steel and the Electric Boat Company in the construction of submarines. For a decade the submarines built by these rivals had vied for the favor of the United States and foreign navies. By 1914, however, Electric Boat was clearly in the lead. The Lake company not only had fewer orders when war broke out but also was saddled with a completed but unsold submarine which had not met a buyer's specifications. The Lake Company was at a further disadvantage because it lacked a salesman to compare with Charles Schwab. Thus, in the same week that Schwab concluded his original contract with the Admiralty for twenty submarines, the Lake Company was reduced to running a large illustrated advertisement in the *Times* of London offering:

FOR SALE—SUBMARINE BOAT AND MINE DESTROYER

Price $300,000 to Governments. Standard Commission to Brokers. Delivery immediately. Several sister craft have been transported across Atlantic upon deck of freighter. Specifications upon request . . . the craft can enter through any mine field and torpedo an enemy's ships within their harbours in spite of shore fortifications.[1]

This offer, complete with its hint of how the neutrality laws of the United States might be evaded, seems to have had no takers, but shortly thereafter the Lake Company did begin discussions with a belligerent government concerning a possible $6,000,000 order for new submarines. At this juncture Secretary of State Bryan announced the apparent cancelation of the Schwab contract. The Lake Company, according to one of its officers, took note of the Schwab affair and found itself "between the conflicting fires of greed and gratitude" to the United States Government for past assistance. "While we felt that we had an unqualified lawful right to ship our product just as had been done in other wars, yet . . . we broke off abruptly negotiations."[2]

Then in February 1915 the officers of the Lake Company read of Ambassador Bernstorff's renewed complaints to the State Department that Schwab was exporting parts of submarines for assembly in Canada. Naturally they were angered. Writing to the State Department, the Company complained that Schwab seemed to be getting special treatment in the form of confiden-

1. *Times* (London) (November 13, 1914).
2. C. E. Adams, secretary of the Lake Torpedo Boat Company, to the Department of State, February 21, 1915, Department of State file 763.72111/1681.

tial information concerning the type of activity which the government was tacitly willing to accept. "We honestly want to help," but ought not the Lake Company be given the same treatment as its competitor? "An inch good naturedly given by the gentle, too often results in a mile gained by the aggressive," wrote the Company in an obvious reference to Bryan and Schwab.[3] In another letter the Company suggested "a friendly test case" on the legality of exporting submarine parts. To prohibit such transactions, the Company argued, would drive a growing industry away from the United States, deprive "many American mechanics" of jobs, and might prevent the United States itself from obtaining submarine parts abroad during an emergency.[4]

Secretary Bryan, in a telegram drafted by Lansing, replied to the Lake company with the same bland assurances given to Bernstorff, that Schwab was not building submarines for delivery to a belligerent. "We appreciate the sentiment in your letter and trust that you will continue to be guided by the feeling of the President that it is really the duty of Americans in the spirit of the rules of neutrality . . . to prevent submarines being shipped from this country, even in parts."[5] The Company was naturally unwilling to accept Bryan's explanation when Schwab's subterfuge was becoming common knowledge. F. B. Whitney, chairman of the board and general counsel, came to Washington on March 6 to discuss the situation with the Department. No written record of what was said has been found, but apparently Whitney obtained a satisfactory explanation. Thereafter the Lake Torpedo Boat Company's fortunes began to improve. By July 1 the Company was operating at full capacity on orders from the United States Navy and, according to the *Wall Street Journal,* from foreign governments.[6]

3. Ibid.
4. H. S. Miller, president of the Company, to the Collector of Customs, port of Bridgeport, Connecticut, February 22, 1915, ibid.
5. Bryan to Lake Torpedo Boat Company, telegram, February 26, 1915, ibid.
6. *Wall Street Journal* (July 1, 1915).

It appears that Whitney of Lake Torpedo received the same verbal definition that had been given to Bethlehem Steel: if exported materials could be assembled into a finished submarine without any further fabrication, then the operation was not acceptable to the government; on the other hand, the government would keep hands off any arrangement whereby the slightest additional manufacturing on the parts outside of the United States was required in order to create a submarine. This interpretation had not yet been committed to writing, but it was gradually becoming widely understood. For example, in April the British ambassador was able to speak confidently of "the American doctrine" that only shipment of *all* essential parts completely manufactured in the United States was a violation of neutrality.[7] This "doctrine," however, was not understood by everyone interested in the affair, as is illustrated by a communication to the Department of State from William Harrison Bradley, the United States Consul-General in Montreal. Bradley reported that his consulate had been visited by "mechanics from the Fall River Iron Works [*sic*] working on submarines being put together at the Vickers-Maxim plant in this city, which, it is understood has been taken over by the Bethlehem Steel Company for that purpose." Managers and men from various Bethlehem plants are in Montreal, Bradley said, and submarines for use in the present war are being completed from parts imported from the United States. "The facts are apparent."[8] Bradley's letter was virtually a challenge to the Department to prevent what he considered a notorious violation of neutrality. Significantly his letter was ignored.

In June 1915 there occurred an event which made possible a clarification of the Department's policy toward submarine parts: Secretary of State Bryan resigned. He left the Department because he disagreed with the character of President Wilson's pro-

7. Spring-Rice to the Governor-General, telegram, April 28, 1915, Borden MSS.

8. Wm. Harrison Bradley to the Secretary of State, May 12, 1915, Department of State file 763.72111/2172.

tests to Germany over the sinking of the *Lusitania*.[9] Wilson, without enthusiasm and because he could think of no one else for the job, appointed Lansing as the new Secretary of State. No longer was it necessary for Lansing to maintain the difficult position of balancing between Bryan and the manufacturers of submarines. Policy could now be stated more openly.

An opportunity for clarification arose in August. The original ten H class submarines for Great Britain were finished and the Canadian Vickers yard was nearly idle. At this point the Electric Boat Company received inquiries concerning submarines from Italy, now a belligerent on the side of the Allies. The possibility was discussed that Bethlehem Steel and Electric Boat might build Italian submarines of the H class under an arrangement similar to that employed for the ten British boats. L. Y. Spear, vice president of Electric Boat, decided that there was too much uncertainty in doing business under an unwritten understanding with the Government. Accordingly Spear asked the Company's attorney in Washington to secure a formal opinion. Spear wrote:

> Our prospective customers ask us to make them a tender upon the greater part of structural steel for the hulls of one or more submarines and desire this material to be delivered in a semi-fabricated form; that is to say, they desire that the transverse frames of the vessel be bent to shape; they also desire that the plating be pressed or furnaced to approximate shape. They do not desire that the vessels be erected in this country and then disassembled for shipment, nor do they desire that any assembly work be done beyond the mere riveting of floor plates to the transverse frames, which is a very minor part of the work involved in the construction of the vessel. . . . by far the greater part of the work involved in building a complete vessel would have to be performed on this material after it reached its destination, fabrication in this country not being carried beyond the preliminary stages. The material as asked for

9. Link, *Wilson*, pp. 419–22.

could not be assembled into a vessel without a great deal of additional work which ordinarily would involve several months' time.[10]

Secretary of State Lansing referred the matter to the Joint State and Navy Neutrality Board, just as he had in the case of the Schwab-Fisher submarines in November 1914. The Board concluded that there was no reason to alter its original decision (there was now no reference to the fact that Bryan and Wilson had taken strong exception to that original decision). "Applying these conclusions to the letter of Mr. Spear . . . the Board sees no objection to the Electric Boat Company undertaking to furnish the component parts of submarines specifically mentioned in that letter, and if the Electric Boat Company does undertake to furnish such material, the Board further believes that the United States has no duty of neutrality in the premises."[11] This time there was no one to appeal over Lansing's head to President Wilson, and it is doubtful whether Wilson was even aware of this new chapter in the history of the submarines. Henceforth Electric Boat's business with belligerents was directly governed by the decision of the Neutrality Board, even as it had been governed in a clandestine fashion previously. In the following months Electric Boat and Bethlehem Steel supplied materials for eight Italian submarines which were completed by Canadian Vickers during 1916. Six H class hulls were also constructed at Canadian Vickers for the Russian government. With these later submarines Canadian Vickers operated its own facilities; they were not leased, as they had been earlier to Bethlehem Steel.

German Ambassador Bernstorff quickly learned of this renewed activity. In September he wrote to Lansing:

I hear that the Union Iron Works of San Francisco are making in their casting and forging shops certain parts for

10. L. Y. Spear, vice president of the Electric Boat Company, to F. E. Chapin, the company's attorney in Washington, August 5, 1915, copy in Department of State file 763.72111/7321.

11. Opinion Number 107 of the Joint State and Navy Neutrality Board, August 10, 1915, ibid.

five submarines that are built at the Schwab works in Montreal. Rudder posts, horizontal rudders, torpedo launching tubes and other various parts are in particular those that are made from drawings of the Electric Boat Company. As those parts are without a doubt intended for war vessels of a belligerent power and will be complete in a few days, I should be obliged to your Excellency if the requisite arrangements were made to prevent exportation of those goods from the United States while the present war endures.[12]

Lansing's response was another round of transparent dissimulation. Schwab was sent a copy of Bernstorff's letter with a request for comment. The reply was exactly as Lansing must have expected:

> In reply . . . I have to say that there are not in Montreal any "Schwab Works" or any works controlled by myself or by any of the companies with which I am associated, nor am I or any of my companies interested in, or connected with, any pending construction of submarines in Montreal or elsewhere in Canada.
>
> As I have advised you in previous communications, the Union Iron Works Company feels free to manufacture, and does manufacture, upon regular commercial orders, forgings and castings and other parts which may be used in the construction of submarines, but its interest in and connection with those products ceases when they are delivered to the customer at our yards.[13]

Lansing, in turn, deemed it sufficient answer to Bernstorff to transmit the substance of Schwab's letter.[14]

While this stereotyped exchange of statements was taking place, the publicity given in the press to the successful crossing of the Atlantic by the submarines from Montreal was producing

12. Bernstorff to Lansing, September 7, 1915, Department of State file 763.72111 E1 1/26.

13. Schwab to Lansing, September 23, 1915, ibid.

14. Lansing to Bernstorff, October 7, 1915, ibid.

unfriendly comment within the Central Powers. From Vienna, American Ambassador Frederick C. Penfield asked the Department of State for help: "In view of President's proclamation of neutrality forbidding construction of equipment of vessels of war for belligerents I should much appreciate statement as to authenticity of report and if correct, the line the Department desires me to take in meeting the criticisms of the Austro-Hungarian Government and public."[15] Two weeks later Ambassador James W. Gerard in Berlin expressed similar uneasiness. "I would be glad to have Department comment as some of highest authorities here are perturbed by report," he cabled.[16] Again Lansing went through the formality of asking Schwab (and the Electric Boat Company) to comment and again received the predictable replies. For the sake of the record Lansing sent identical telegrams to the ambassadors in Vienna and Berlin: "After investigation Department finds no evidence that any submarines have been built in the United States for delivery during the present war, or that any submarines have left American jurisdiction under their own power."[17] After receiving the telegram, Penfield presented a formal statement in the same sense to the Austro-Hungarian Foreign Office.[18] Exactly one year had passed since Schwab's initial conversation with Lord Fisher in the Admiralty. Thus ended the submarine affair as far as protests from foreign governments were concerned.[19]

15. Penfield to Lansing (via Berne), telegram, October 15, 1915, Department of State file 763.72111 E1 1/29.

16. Gerard to Lansing (via Copenhagen), telegram, October 29, 1915, Department of State file 763.72111 E1 1/54.

17. Lansing to Penfield, November 1, 1915, and to Gerard, November 3, 1915, ibid.

18. Penfield to Lansing, November 12, 1915, enclosing copy of memorandum of November 9, 1915 which he presented to the Austro-Hungarian Foreign Office, Department of State file 763.72111 E1 1/39.

19. Bernstorff did advert to the submarines again in a letter to Lansing, November 28, 1915, but Lansing ignored the comments. See *Foreign Relations of the United States, 1915*, pp. 818–20; and also Charles C. Tansill, *America Goes to War* (Boston, 1938), p. 47, n. 54. Finally, it should be noted that the Department of State files (763.72111/1548) contain an interesting document dated December 29, 1916, on the submarines. It is a copy of a code telegram, with interlinear translation, from Bruce Bielaski, head of the

So far, we have been concerned exclusively with the circumstances surrounding the *construction* of the ten Schwab submarines. A word about their war record might be interesting. They played an active role, considering the limited opportunities open to British submarines in a war where the enemy seldom sent ships into the open seas. After their launching in Montreal, the submarines moved down the St. Lawrence; some finishing touches were applied at Quebec and trials were conducted off Murray Bay in the early summer of 1915.[20] In England the Admiralty had decided to assign six of the new submarines to home waters as an additional safeguard against German invasion. (In a meeting of the War Council at 10 Downing Street on May 14, 1915, Lord Kitchener said he thought there was a possibility of German attack. Churchill, disagreeing, said that the imminent arrival of the new submarines and some destroyers meant that "there was absolutely no need for anxiety.")[21] The six, H 5 to H 10, crossed the Atlantic in July and began a series of defensive patrols. Subsequently H 6 became stranded on the Dutch coast and was interned by the Royal Netherlands Navy.[22]

Secret Service in the Treasury Department, to a treasury agent in San Francisco. The telegram summarizes the correspondence exchanged between the Department of State and Schwab during 1915 and concludes: "State Department has taken position that shipment castings, gears, et cetera, not unlawful. Not desired this information be made public unless judgment . . . essential best interests government this case." It seems probable that this telegram had something to do with the continuing connection of the Union Iron Works in San Francisco with submarine work at Canadian Vickers. It is also significant that the Department of State, as late as December 1916, should be concerned to conceal the nature of the unwritten agreement by which the Schwab exports to Canada were made.

20. Tucker, *Naval Service, I*, 235.

21. Secretary's Notes of a Meeting of a War Council held at 10 Downing Street, May 14, 1915, Asquith MSS, box 132.

22. R. H. Gibson and Maurice Prendergast, *The German Submarine War, 1914–1918* (London, 1931), p. 83. A year after the first H boats crossed the Atlantic without public fanfare, the famous German cargo-carrying submarine *Deutschland* visited the United States and received wide but misinformed acclaim as the first submarine to cross the Atlantic under its own power. There were fifty-two boats in the entire H class, all ordered during the First World War. Ten were completed in Canada, ten in the United

The other four, H 1 to H 4, went initially to the Dardanelles, where British submarines of the E class (built by Vickers in Great Britain from Electric Boat designs) had already been successfully engaged and where the British commanding officer, Sir Ian Hamilton, was tireless in his demands for as many submarines as the Admiralty could spare.[23] The four H's arrived near Gallipoli in October 1915 and immediately went into action. The exploits of the H 1, in particular, were spectacular, according to a letter written by her commander, Lt. W. B. Pirie:

> We are the first submarine in history to bombard a place on shore under fire. I think we were under fire on an average three times a day and penetrated into all sorts of places and destroyed shipping. We even shelled a railway and destroyed two troop trains. We shelled an embankment and blocked the line, then caught the trains as they came along. It was the funniest thing you can imagine to see the train try to hide between the trees, but we caught her and smashed her to blazes. Three ammunition wagons blew up with terrific explosions. The soldiers, of course, got out and took cover and fired tons of ammunition at us, but we were out of range. Altogether we sank 1 gunboat, 5 steamers (one of 3,000 tons), and 17 large sailing ships, and destroyed three trains and one railway embankment.[24]

States, and thirty-two in Great Britain. Eight of them (although none built in Canada) survived to see active service during the Second World War. I am indebted to Canadian Vickers, Ltd., for this information.

The H boats were 150 feet long and had a displacement tonnage of 357. For the sake of comparison, the nuclear ballistic missile submarine *Daniel Webster*, built by the Electric Boat Division of General Dynamics and commissioned at Groton, Connecticut, April 9, 1964, is 425 feet long and displaces 7,000 tons. Information supplied by the General Dynamics Corporation.

23. The decision to send the four H's to the Dardanelles was made at a meeting of the Dardanelles Committee at 10 Downing Street on June 7, 1915; see the minutes of the meeting, Asquith MSS, box 132. For Hamilton's views see his letter of September 2, 1915, ibid., box 8.

24. House of Representatives, Naval Affairs Committee, *Hearings, 1916*, 2, 1699, quoting Pirie's letter as printed in the London *Evening Mail* (February 3, 1916).

Later in the war the H 1 and the H 4 each sank another submarine. The H 1's victim, unfortunately, belonged to Britain's ally, Italy, and was in fact one of the H class submarines built at Canadian Vickers in 1916. The H 4, however, sank the German UB 52 off the Dalmatian coast late in May 1918.[25] Six months later the war was over.

The story of the clandestine submarines would not be complete without an account of the ten submarines, of the original contract for twenty, which were not built in Montreal. Under the supplementary contract between Schwab and the Admiralty, following Bryan's intervention against the first contract, it was agreed that the construction of the second ten would continue in the United States. Because of the "diplomatic situation" the method and date of delivery was left undecided. Schwab's profits, however, were secure in all contingencies. Even if the submarines were held in the United States for delivery after the war the Admiralty agreed to pay $600,000 each.

Through the winter and spring of 1915 work on the second ten submarines proceeded at the Fore River Shipbuilding Company while the first ten were being finished and launched in Montreal. The State Department, kept fully informed of the work at Fore River, watched carefully. As a precaution against the possible escape of the submarines from American jurisdiction (an event rumored from time to time in the press), naval officers acting under orders from the Secretary of the Navy were on board during sea trials in September 1915.[26] Immediately after the trials (which were successful), the ten submarines were placed under the custody of the Commandant of the Boston Navy Yard.[27] The spirit and letter of the *Alabama* decision were being zealously met.

For a year the submarines lay thus impounded. Meanwhile changing circumstances fast diminished their potential useful-

25. Gibson and Prendergast, *German Submarine War*, p. 268.
26. Secretary of the Navy Josephus Daniels to Lansing, September 4, 1915, Department of State files 763.72111/2830.
27. Daniels to Lansing, January 6, 1917, Department of State files 763.72111/4397.

ness to the British. Lord Fisher had long since departed from a position of influence. The Dardanelles operation had been ignominiously abandoned in failure. British shipbuilders were producing more submarines than the Admiralty knew how to use. The only submarines that mattered now belonged to Germany.

Although the Admiralty had written off the impounded vessels, the Foreign Office, in September 1916, discovered a use for some of them: five were offered as a gift to neutral Chile. Since the outbreak of war in August 1914 Chile had felt resentment against Great Britain because of interference with the Chilean naval building program in Britain. One nearly finished dreadnought, the *Almirante,* had been requisitioned for the Royal Navy (and renamed, by coincidence, the *Canada*).[28] Some smaller vessels had also been taken over, while others, including a second dreadnought, were left incomplete, their construction suspended for the duration of the war. An additional irritant had been the pre-emption by the province of British Columbia of the two submarines which were, at the outbreak of war, in Seattle awaiting acceptance by Chile.[29] Thus in 1916 a gift of the submarines, which were unavailable for direct British use, seemed an excellent way of partially assuaging Chilean resentment.

Initially Foreign Secretary Sir Edward Grey told Chile that the submarines could not be delivered until the end of the war. The Chilean Minister in London complained, however, that the end of the war was too indefinite a date to be acceptable. Chile also asked for a sixth submarine to be purchased beyond the five gifts. After Grey consulted Arthur Balfour, Churchill's successor as First Lord of the Admiralty, Chile was promised that the submarines (including a sixth purchased vessel) would be delivered no later than June 8, 1917, whether or not the war was over. When the British made that promise the American government became involved.

28. See Asquith to the King, September 5, 1914, reporting on Cabinet decisions of September 3 and 4, Asquith MSS, box 7.
29. See above, pp. 20–21.

Secretary of State Lansing learned of the Anglo-Chilean arrangement in November 1916 when Joseph H. Shea, the American minister in Santiago, cabled full details.[30] Lansing, suspicious, replied to Shea that the United States might be impelled to prevent the transaction on the grounds that it was a ruse by which the British might take over Chilean warships under construction in Britain. This would be tantamount to allowing the British government to acquire six of the impounded submarines, something which would violate American neutrality.[31]

In Santiago the Chilean Foreign Minister was resentful of Lansing's insinuation. He explained excitedly to the American minister that "the transfer of the five submarines is a compensation offered by the British Government and accepted by us for the serious damages caused by the delay in the delivery of our ships." The only warship still under construction for Chile in Britain was a dreadnought upon which almost no work was being done. No arrangement had been made or would be made to transfer that vessel to the British government.[32]

These assurances diluted Lansing's suspicions. Would Chile be willing, Lansing asked, to make an explicit pledge that the submarines were for the use of Chile alone and that they would not be transferred to any of the belligerents during the present war? The Secretary said this pledge was necessary to disarm criticism which was expected to arise "in certain quarters" the moment the submarines left American waters.[33] The pledge was readily given,[34] and in January 1917 the Commandant of the Boston Navy Yard transferred six of the ten impounded submarines to the Fore River Shipbuilding Company, which, in turn, handed them over to Chile.[35]

30. Shea to Lansing, telegram, November 2, 1916, Department of State file 763.72111/4227.
31. Lansing to Shea, telegram, November 10, 1916, ibid.
32. Shea to Lansing, telegram, November 16, 1916, ibid., /4244; and despatch, November 19, 1916, ibid., /4328.
33. Lansing to Shea, telegram, November 20, 1916, ibid., /4244.
34. Shea to Lansing, telegram, November 29, 1916, ibid., /4288.
35. Daniels to Lansing, January 6, 1917, ibid., /4397.

Four submarines remained. After the entry of the United States into the war in April 1917 no legal obstacle stood in the way of their delivery to Great Britain; however, they did not actually cross the Atlantic until the autumn of 1918. As early as May 1915, it will be recalled, the Admiralty had suggested that Canada might wish to purchase two of the then-impounded submarines for delivery after the war.[36] In January 1919 the suggestion was renewed, although this time the submarines were offered to Canada as a gift. Sir Robert Borden, in Paris for the Peace Conference, consulted his colleagues in Ottawa and accepted. "The two submarines, H 14 and H 15, arrived at Halifax in June and were commissioned in the Royal Canadian Navy as CH 14 and CH 15."[37] The last remaining pair were scrapped in 1919 by the Admiralty. The history of the clandestine submarines was over.

36. See above, pp. 109–10.
37. Tucker, *Naval Service,* p. 317.

10 The Submarines and the Triangle: Some Reflections

In the twentieth century the United States, Canada, and Great Britain have blended resources in the interests of their separate and collective security. Since the Second World War their cooperation has explicitly involved all three governments in common objectives. But during the Great War the United States remained neutral for more than two and a half years; the objective of the American government was to keep out of the war. Can we claim, therefore, that a triangular process of cooperation existed before the American declaration of war on Germany in April 1917?

The submarine episode suggests that there was a genuine Triangle, although it was tenuous, incomplete, frequently ignored, and just as frequently misunderstood. The one man truly aware of it in the submarine episode was Charles M. Schwab, whose imagination and experience in the international steel and armaments industry enabled him to transcend national boundaries in his thinking. Thanks to Schwab's ingenuity the submarines were produced by the combined resources of the Triangle, notwithstanding the largely negative and ill-informed behavior of the three governments concerned. Canada was in this case a link between the United States and Great Britain, but the link was the result of individual initiative, geographical convenience, and industrial development within the three countries; it was not the result of deliberate policy by one or more of the governments. Canada by her presence served to facilitate the application of the resources of a neutral United States to the war against the Central Powers.

Upon reflection, one of the most noteworthy aspects of the affair is the degree to which government officials in the three countries ignored or misunderstood the triangular process taking place under their gaze. Not one of the political figures fully comprehended the network of close relationships which produced the submarines with such remarkable speed and efficiency. Some comments on the diagram following page 92 will illustrate the intricate nature of this network.

By 1914 nearly all submarines produced outside of Germany utilized vital parts the patents of which were owned by the Electric Boat Company in the United States·and assigned under a license to Vickers, Ltd., in Great Britain. Before the outbreak of war Vickers, through loans and heavy stock purchases, had kept the Electric Boat Company alive during several lean years for the submarine business in the United States.

The Vickers-Electric Boat axis was tied, in turn, to Canada by means of Canadian Vickers, a wholly owned subsidiary of the British parent company. Any naval shipbuilding by the Canadian company would require assistance from Britain in the form of plans, specialized parts, higher management, and skilled shipbuilding labor—at least such was the expectation for the contracts from the Admiralty which never materialized between 1911 and 1914. With the submarines, of course, these special services and materials came instead from the United States.

The trans-Atlantic network included the Bethlehem Steel Corporation, largest naval shipbuilding concern in the United States at that time, through an arrangement whereby Electric Boat and its subsidiary, the New London Ship and Engine Company, produced submarine engines and parts which Bethlehem used in the construction of submarines at either of its subsidiaries: the Fore River Shipbuilding Company in Quincy, Massachusetts, and the Union Iron Works in San Francisco. Incidentally, the lasting nature of the ties between Bethlehem

Steel and the Electric Boat Company are illustrated by Bethlehem's decision to sell the Fore River yard to the General Dynamics Corporation in 1964. After the sale the Electric Boat
Division of General Dynamics planned to build surface vessels
at the Quincy facility. (*New York Times,* December 7 and 15,
1963.)

Under the original contract between Schwab and the Admiralty all work on the submarines was to be done in the United
States. After the intervention by the American government,
however, Schwab had no difficulty employing the network of
relationships which already existed in order to circumvent the
apparent consequences of the administration's action. Vickers,
Ltd., readily complied with the request of its major customer,
the Admiralty, and made the Canadian Vickers plant available
for Schwab. The necessary men and materials moved north to
Montreal. American and Canadian laborers went to work and
soon the submarines were launched: the result of a smooth
supranational process within the Triangle.

In contrast to Schwab, the political figures in the affair were
narrowly national in their patterns of thought. This was especially true of Prime Minister Borden. He considered Canadian
Vickers a separate, independent national company, a tribute to
the Dominion's status, not a mere externally controlled branch.
Influenced by the ambitious claims of Canadian Vickers executives and swayed by his own dreams of what Canada might become, Borden believed the company fully capable of producing
warships without external assistance. Therefore, the failure of
the Admiralty to place contracts directly with Canadian Vickers
was an affront to his national pride. When the facilities of
Canadian Vickers were ultimately used by an American corporation, the affront became almost unbearable. So primary was
the appeal of national interests—of jobs, prestige, and industrial growth for Canada—that Borden derived only slight
comfort from the realization that the submarines, after all, were
completed and that they did contribute to the defense of the
Empire.

Officials of the British government also failed to comprehend the nature of the Triangle. Borden exaggerated Canada's economic maturity, confusing the future with the present; but Churchill and Fisher, confusing the past with the present, were backward in their concept of the Dominion's capabilities. Canada's persistent demands for naval shipbuilding contracts were regarded as a nuisance. The overriding concern of the Admiralty was naturally for the most rapid delivery of submarines from whatever source. No allowances for Canadian sensitivity could be made if they might impede the acquisition of the submarines. In time of war it is often necessary for a government to disregard local interests within the nation. The British government erred, however, in acting, during the early stages of the war, as if Canadian interests were local, British, and to a degree expendable. Men like Churchill failed to understand the extent to which Canadian behavior in the war was motivated by Canadian national conditions and not general British interests. Churchill's British nationalism blinded him to its Canadian counterpart. Because of this blindness he, and many others in Britain, did not succeed in the first years of the war in commanding Canada's maximum support materially or psychologically in the war effort. Lloyd George from December 1916 onward did better.

Members of the American government likewise did not grasp the triangular relationship in which the facilities for the production of submarines were meshed. Lansing was less oblivious to the process than Bryan or Wilson, but all three shared an ignorance of Canada even greater than that found within the British government. The Americans also, insofar as they thought of Canada at all, conceived of the Dominion as she once had been, not as she was becoming. For these men the contract for submarines between Schwab and the Admiralty raised a question of neutrality involving the United States bilaterally with Great Britain. Wilson, in particular, did not conceive of Canada as politically separate from Great Britain. For him the Dominion was a non-self-governing colony, a subdivision of the British Empire with scarcely more independence than an English county.

As the Great War progressed, however, the undeniable presence of the triangular process wrought a variety of changes
in the outlook and understanding of the political leaders within
the three nations. A full discussion of these changes is far
beyond the compass of the present study; yet it is significant
that the majority of the changes were, in effect, responses to
the unsatisfactory conditions which the episode of the submarines so vividly represented. Each passing month of war
brought further stimulus to Canadian national feeling. Indeed,
the correspondence, diaries, and other writings of Canadians of
the time are so imbued with a rising tone of national self-
assertion that one is sometimes tempted to say that the conflict
was, incidentally, a war for Canadian independence. Certainly
the gallant sacrifices of Canada's soldiers provided the principal
impetus to this sense of nationhood, but bread-and-butter economic issues symbolized by the submarines were of great importance also. Specifically in shaping the attitudes of members
of the Canadian government episodes like the submarine affair
may have played a larger role than the less immediate but more
emotional sacrifice of men in battle.

Gradually the British government, thanks in part to changes
in personnel from the spring of 1915 on, came to appreciate
the intensity of Canadian national feeling and the seriousness
of the ever-louder insistence from Ottawa that Canada's voice
be heeded. Englishmen wisely accepted and suggested methods
for giving Canada a greater economic, military, and political
role—most notably through the establishment of the Imperial
Munitions Board and the Imperial War Cabinet. Had Britain
failed to do these things—had there occurred an unending
series of submarine episodes through 1916 and 1917, for example—the outcome would have been unfortunate for the
cause of the Triangle in the Great War. During the second
half of the war Anglo-Canadian cooperation and Canada's contribution to the war were at their peak precisely because the
British Government had gone far to acknowledge and even encourage the national distinctiveness of Canada. Paradoxically,
unity and independence grew apace.

It is less easy to generalize about what the submarine affair suggests concerning the position of the United States in the Triangle. The affair represented one of the many ways in which Canada exerted an influence on American neutrality. As many men in Britain and the United States came to realize, Canada was an alternative site for North American production. If special circumstances such as an American embargo on the shipment of munitions had seriously threatened to deprive the Allies of the direct productive facilities of the United States, it would not have been difficult for American manufacturers to have emulated Schwab by switching operations to Canada. As the perceptive and pro-British James Brown Scott of the Joint State and Navy Neutrality Board observed in 1915 in a letter to Theodore Roosevelt:

> if the United States should put an embargo upon the exportation of arms, American workmen would undoubtedly go over to Canada, where they would be employed in factories, and the Administration would thus by its action tend to create a rivalry to the north of us. American farmers of the Northwest have gone in thousands and tens of thousands to Canada, attracted by the wheat fields of that region. It is not to be doubted that a resourceful statesman of the type of the Right Honorable Lloyd George [at that time British Minister of Munitions] would avail himself of this opportunity of building up Canadian manufactures, and that in the course of his speech in Parliament he would express the pleasure it gave the mother country to aid the loyal Canadians in building up their industries.[1]

Years later, in a similar vein, Thomas Lamont, of J. P. Morgan and Company, testified before the Nye Committee that the availability of Canada gave the British a lever by which they could obtain better terms in their financial negotiations with American bankers who dared not be too demanding, "unless

1. James Brown Scott to Theodore Roosevelt, July 26, 1915, Theodore Roosevelt MSS.

they were prepared to see the British Government change in its whole attitude on purchasing and try to get their goods in Canada. That was always in the background."[2]

Actually, the very fact that the Wilson Administration reversed its initial ban and allowed American bankers to make loans to belligerents was in part the result of Canada's presence as a real and potential competitor. Lansing succeeded, in October 1914, in convincing Wilson to modify the ban, and did so by using arguments provided by the banking community that "otherwise the buying power of these foreign purchasers will dry up and the business will go to Australia, Canada, Argentine and elsewhere. . . . we will have neglected our foreign trade at the time of our . . . greatest opportunity."[3]

In addition to this industrial and financial influence, Canada provided a convenient destination for the thousands of Americans who enlisted voluntarily in the war against Germany. The activities of these individuals were thoroughly and approvingly publicized by the American press and were often described as symbolizing the sympathy of the American people—as contrasted with the cold neutrality of the government—with the Allied cause. Had Canada not existed, it would have been far more difficult for volunteers, especially men without funds, to have enlisted from the United States.

The episode of the submarines, when considered in the light of these other factors, suggests that the bearing of Canada on American neutrality was greater than historians have acknowledged. Certainly more research is needed. Without Canada the United States might still have gone to war against Germany. Who can speak with confidence about an untestable hypothesis? But it is undeniable that Canada was a major force inclining the material interests and sympathy of Americans toward the Allied side. The United States went to war more readily because of the triangular process. By the spring of 1917 the policies of the government of the United States began to conform

2 U.S. Senate, *Hearings before the Special Senate Committee on the Investigation of the Munitions Industry,* 74th Congress, 2d Session, 25, 7626–27.

3. *Foreign Relations of the United States: The Lansing Papers, 1,* 139.

far more closely to the pattern of relationships within the North Atlantic Triangle than had been the case upon the outbreak of the war.

The greater understanding of the Triangle which appeared in 1917 and 1918 did not fade away entirely after the Armistice. When the second great crisis of defense confronted the triangle two decades later, the relationship which had been tenuous, incomplete, and characterized by ill feeling and subterfuge in 1914 and 1915 was openly proclaimed by the three governments. The gap between the comprehension of the politicians and the reality of the Triangle was less. The contrast between Woodrow Wilson and Franklin D. Roosevelt and between the episode of the clandestine submarines and the mutual defense arrangements which grew up immediately after 1939 are measures of change within the North Atlantic Triangle in this century.

A Note on the Sources

The first step in the preparation of this monograph was both the most difficult and the most pleasurable: the search for sources on an episode about which little had been written and the ramifications of which had never before been understood, even by the participants at the time. The sources—principally in the form of manuscript materials embedded in tons of records on the Great War in three countries—were gathered over a period of three years in libraries, archives, and collections of personal papers in Canada, the United States, and Great Britain.

The most important single collection was the Papers of Sir Robert Borden in the magnificent Public Archives of Canada in Ottawa. The Borden Papers constitute one of the richest sources anywhere for twentieth-century Canadian and Atlantic Triangle political history. They contain several hundred documents on the submarine affair. The Canadian side of the story could not be told without them. The Papers of Sir George Perley, Sir John Willison, Sir Joseph Flavelle, and Sir Joseph Pope, also in the Public Archives of Canada, provided significant tangential details. Records, photographs, and information supplied by Canadian Vickers, Ltd., Montreal, were indispensable, as was a personal visit to the company's shipyard, many features of which have not changed since 1915. Also of use was the Diary of Sir Robert Borden in the possession of Henry Borden, Esquire, Toronto, when I consulted it, but which is now in the Public Archives in Ottawa.

On the American side the single most important collection of unpublished material was the files of the Department of State in the Diplomatic, Legal, and Fiscal Branch of the National Archives, Washington, especially files 763.72111/ and 763.72111 E1 1/. The portion of the William Jennings Bryan Papers in the National Archives also yielded some fragments of information, as did records in the Navy Branch of the Archives. In the Division of Manuscripts, Library of Congress, Washington, the Papers of Robert Lansing, especially the desk diary with its meticulous notation of hourly appointments, were most useful, while the Chandler Anderson Papers, the William Jennings Bryan Papers, the Wilbur J. Carr Papers, the Josephus Daniels Papers, the Theodore Roosevelt Papers, and the Woodrow Wilson Papers all produced small bits of material valuable in filling out the context of the story. The same may be said for the Diary and Papers of Colonel Edward M. House in the Yale University Library, New Haven, Connecticut. The two most important single documents for the entire study—the original and supplementary contracts between the British Admiralty and the Bethlehem Steel Corporation—were furnished in photostatic copies from the Bethlehem Steel Archives, South Bethlehem, Pennsylvania. The Archives of the Electric Boat Division of the General Dynamics Corporation at the Submarine Library, Groton, Connecticut, contained information unavailable elsewhere and confirmed some things that were unclear in other sources.

In Great Britain the Papers of Admiral Lord Fisher in possession of the Duke of Hamilton, Lennoxlove, Haddington, Scotland, and the Papers of Prime Minister Herbert H. Asquith, the Bodleian Library, Oxford University, Oxford, were indispensable for information on the British side of the episode. The records of Vickers, Ltd., Vickers House, London; the Papers of Lord Bryce in the Bodleian; and the Papers of Sir Edward Grey and Sir Cecil Spring-Rice in the Foreign Office Library all contained details ranging from the essential to the useful.

There is little documentary material on the submarine episode in print with the exception of the correspondence included in the Department of State, *Papers Relating to the Foreign Relations of the United States: 1914, Supplement, The World War* (Washington, 1928); ibid., *1915, Supplement, The World War* (1928); and ibid., *The Lansing Papers, 1914–1920* (2 vols. Washington, 1939–40). The *Congressional Record,* the *Debates of the House of Commons* in Canada and in Great Britain, the Canadian Government's *Labour Gazette,* and the *Hearings of the House Naval Affairs Committee* and *Hearings before the Special Senate Committee on the Investigation of the Munitions Industry* (Nye Committee) all supplied some background material.

Newspapers frequently contained details unavailable elsewhere. The *Wall Street Journal* was surprisingly full of comment, often quite accurate, on the submarines. The *Montreal Daily Star* was useful for background conditions in Montreal and for details on the beginnings of the arrangement with Canadian Vickers (later the British Government's insistence on secrecy prevented Canadian papers from reporting on the submarines). The *New York Times* and the *Times* (London) also produced important details, as did the San Francisco *Examiner* and the San Francisco *Chronicle.*

Although it is impossible to discover very much about the submarines from secondary sources, historians, biographers, and memoirists have mentioned the affair on several occasions—but always briefly, inaccurately, or both. For example, Winston S. Churchill's *The World Crisis* (New York, 1923) prints some important documents on the Admiralty's search for more submarines in the autumn of 1914, but his narrative is riddled with minor errors. In writing of Schwab's first visit to the Admiralty in November 1914, Churchill says (p. 497), "Mr. Schwab was at that time passing through England on his return to the United States. We invited him to the Admiralty; and he undertook to build twenty-four submarines—twelve in Canada and twelve in the United States . . . ." In those few words Churchill makes three errors: (1) Schwab was not "passing through," he had come to England specifically to solicit munitions contracts; (2) he undertook to build twenty, not twenty-four submarines; (3) he planned to build them all in the United States (the second contract following Wilson's and Bryan's intervention provided for the completion of ten vessels in Canada). Admittedly these are not major errors, but their number is an object lesson for the scholar who would rely on the subsequently printed word rather than the documents generated by the event at the time.

The most recent mention of the submarines is by Arthur S. Link, in *Wilson: The Struggle for Neutrality, 1914–1915* (Princeton, 1960), pp. 61–62. But Link deals with the affair only up to December 1914; after describing Bryan's announcement of Schwab's promise, he writes, "As the Secretary observed . . . the 'submarine incident' was closed." Charles Callan Tansill, an earlier and more caustic, if less objective, chronicler of American neutrality, was aware of the Canadian continuation of the episode, but his account in *America Goes to War* (Boston, 1938), pp. 42–48, is part conjecture and is unconvincingly documented.

For the background of Canadian naval policy, the first volume of Gilbert Norman Tucker's *The Naval Service of Canada* (2 vols. Ottawa, 1952) is workmanlike, although it gives insufficient emphasis to the Canadian government's deep interest in the development of a naval shipbuilding industry in Canada. On British naval affairs in the decade before the war, Arthur J. Marder's *From the Dreadnought to Scapa Flow*, Vol. I, *The Road to War, 1904–1914* (London, 1961) is superb, an incomparable example of exhaustive historical research, brilliant writing, and broad interpretations. Professor Marder's book is the first half of a projected study, *The Royal Navy in the Fisher Era, 1904–1919*.

Finally, from a mass of literature on the Great War, I would single out the following for their explicit comments on or their immediate relevance to the episode of the submarines: Volume 5 of Ray Stannard Baker's *Woodrow Wilson: Life and Letters* (8 vols. Garden City, 1927–39); Henry Borden, ed., *Robert Laird Borden: His Memoirs* (2 vols. Toronto, 1938), diffuse and poorly organized; Sir Douglas Brownrigg's *Indiscretions of a*

Naval Censor (New York, 1920), for a colorful glimpse of Schwab at the Admiralty; Admiral Lord Fisher, *Memories and Records* (2 vols. New York, 1920) for his account of the first interview with Schwab; Eugene Gifford Grace's *Charles M. Schwab* (n.p., 1947), a reminiscence by a Bethlehem Steel executive who knew Schwab intimately; Admiral Lord Jellicoe in *The Grand Fleet, 1914–16* (New York, 1919), tells of meeting Schwab on the *Olympic* on the occasion of the sinking of the *Audacious;* also Arthur J. Marder, ed., *Fear God and Dreadnought: The Correspondence of Admiral of the Fleet Lord Fisher of Kilverstone* (3 vols. London, 1952–59); John Niven, et al., *Dynamic America: A History of the General Dynamics Corporation* (New York, 1958), for excellent photographs of the submarines and their parts in shipment; Charles M. Schwab's *Succeeding with What You Have* (New York, 1917), for what it reveals of his personality, and J. D. Scott, *Vickers: A History* (London, 1963) for its fascinating account of the development of one of the world's largest armaments manufacturers.

Index